RAISING
God's Girl

Empowering Parents
to Raise Daughters
with Conviction,
Confidence
& Courage

Rich and Mary Lou
GRAHAM

RAISING GOD'S GIRL

Cover Design by Jessica Brice

FIRST EDITION

ISBN: 978-0-9962716-9-1

Library of Congress Control Number: 2015947906

Published by

P.O. Box 2839, Apopka, FL 32704

Printed in the United States of America

Disclaimer: The views and opinions expressed in this book are solely those of the authors and other contributors. These views and opinions do not necessarily represent those of Certa Publishing.

Dedication

Dear Brittany, Becky, Katie, and Stephanie,

We thank you for your love, your patience, your forgiveness, and your willingness to share your lives with us. You have filled our home and our hearts with laugher and joy. We have thanked God through the sunshine and learned to cling to Him during the storms. We are eternally grateful to God for each one of you. You are far better than we deserve!

We love you,

Mom and Dad

RAISING GOD'S GIRL

Thanks to Sarah S., Jessica, Christina, Grace, Cynthia, Sarah K., Abby, Ruth, and Toshiko. You have laughed with us, cried with us, and shared life with us. We love you like daughters. Our home and our lives are richer because of you.

CONTENTS

LET'S TALK

Do you think it's difficult to raise girls today? Stores hang up scraps of material and try to pass them off as bathing suits. Music blares throughout the mall glorifying violence against women. Teachers dole out sexual advice and technique suggestions. Potential suitors spend their days engrossed in sports and video games. Vicious slander is rampant on social media. Movies mock the dufus dad and turn the rebellious girl into a hero when she disobeys her father. And a young girl needs parental permission to have her ear pierced, but she is allowed to have an abortion without her parents being informed. Something is wrong here!

If you are reading this book, we are assuming two things:

1. You have a daughter that you deeply love and want to raise her to know the Lord and be secure in His love instead of falling into the trappings of the world. You want your daughter to live a bold, passionate, Godward life and follow the Lord Jesus Christ whole-heartedly, trusting Him to lead her every step of the way.
2. You are a busy parent and would appreciate that we respect your time by sharing honestly, specifically, and candidly.

If this describes you, then you've got the right book.

So let's imagine together...after meeting you at a conference and having great conversations, we decide to get together again. Responsible babysitters have been secured, and we are all looking forward to a night of "grown-up" talk and fellowship.

We meet at a local café and order coffee, hot tea, and desserts. The atmosphere is relaxing as we catch up on news about each other's families. You pull out your smart phone and show us pictures of your wonderful children, and we rejoice with you as we look at your beautiful blessings from God.

We pull out our own smart phones and show you pictures of Joey (9), Johnny (12), Stephen (14), Stephanie (16), Katie (18), and Becky (22). We then show you a picture of Brittany (25) glowing from pregnancy and surrounded by her husband, Daniel, the young boy they are fostering (2), and their birth son (1). You also rejoice with us, and then the conversation flows easily into the topic of parenting. We quickly focus on a specific issue that's challenging all of us in today's culture: raising our girls to know that they're God's girls.

That's where this book picks up. We are fellow parents who love Jesus and want to raise our daughters for Him and want to help other parents to do the same. We ask you to be gracious in your reading of this book, knowing that we have our daughters' permission to share stories about them, and we have their full support in wanting to encourage other families on this mission.

Listening to Our Daughters

In fact, our daughters helped us write this book. We all know communication is composed of two parts: the message sent and the message received. We as parents may think we are communicating the right message, but it is insightful to look into the hearts of young ladies and learn what words and actions actually convey love and encouragement for godly living. Joy Dawson does a masterful job of this in her book *Influencing Children to Become World Changers*, as she includes testimonies from her children and grandchildren. Her teaching is rich, and the reflections from her family are priceless.[1]

So we thought it might be helpful if our four daughters shared their thoughts with you. At the end of each chapter, you will find a section called "The Daughters Speak." We hope you will be encouraged by these candid glimpses into their hearts as we see family life through the eyes of young girls.

Learning from Books

We whole-heartedly believe that the Bible is the only perfect book. No other book is perfect, including the one in your hand. As committed Christians, we are called to raise our children according to the truths in the Bible. There are uncompromising truths that must be taught and followed. To be a Christian means to be a follower of Christ, and therefore we do not have the freedom, or wisdom, to make up our own guidelines for life or for parenting. If we are looking for the Lord to bless our parenting efforts, we should raise our children according to His instructions. We must embrace the truths in Scripture and cry out for wisdom as to how to implement them in our homes and in our lives.

To compromise in this is to commit a great disservice to our children. When we read a parenting book, it is easy to struggle in one of two ways. First, when we come across teaching that challenges us to raise our vision and standards, we can instantly dismiss the authors as too legalistic, too perfect, too…something. Instead of recognizing our weaknesses and learning from the biblical counsel of others, we quickly dismiss the advice as "not for us."

Another way to struggle when reading a parenting book is on the opposite extreme. We read scripturally based advice, and we fall into despair. We could never be parents like that; we could never be that faithful; we could never be that diligent. And we close the book, left with no hope.

Have you heard this phrase: "The devil doesn't care what side of the horse you fall off, as long as you fall off?" Our enemy doesn't care what keeps us from applying God's principles to our parenting; he cares only that we stay far away from biblical encouragement and obedience.

So, please read this like we should read all parenting books: First, check the principles taught to make sure they line up with Scripture. Second, read with faith that God will speak to you personally. Something that we share may spark an idea in you. Write it down. It may be completely off the topic of what you're reading; just write it down. Write all over the margins of this book. Highlight. Record the thoughts and ideas that God speaks to you specifically for your unique family.

Let's Talk Spiritual...and Practical

We share many examples from our family. Why? Because that's the type of advice we like to get...practical. We once had friends with a house full of children that served the Lord. I (Mary Lou) was excited when an opportunity arose to speak to the mother alone, and I asked her what things she has implemented in her home that have been especially helpful. A young mother myself, I eagerly waited for her response as she hesitated. Finally she replied that she couldn't really think of anything, but that God had just helped her through it all.

I came away disappointed. Yes, we know God is our only hope for fruitful parenting. Yes, our children belong to Him. Yes, we need to cling to Him for the strength to lead our children. Yes, yes, yes. But parenting is a verb! And placing the word *biblical* in front of it is not just adding an adjective; it is defining parenting with an enormous mandate: biblical. Biblical parenting is actively and intentionally raising *God's* girl in *His* way, with *His* power—for *His* purposes. The calling is huge! The opposition is fierce! And the results are eternal!

So let's talk spiritual. Let's talk practical. And let's talk with power and faith. He who begins a good work in our children will be faithful to complete it (Phil. 1:6). Let's jump in to what God is doing!

Prayer

Heavenly Father, please give me wisdom to raise my daughter for Your glory. I want her to be secure in Your love. I want her to know Jesus and the power of His resurrection and to follow Him all the days of her life, turning her back on the things of the world. Please speak to me through this book and help me to know what You want me to do as a result of what I learn. Help me to be faithful to do everything You want me to do.

---

1 Joy Dawson, *Influencing Your Children to Become World Changers* (Nashville: Thomas Nelson, Inc., 2003).

1

That's God's Girl!

Cherishing Your Gift from God

"I will give thanks to You, for I am fearfully and wonderfully made; wonderful are Your works, and my soul knows it very well" (Ps. 139:14). We've seen this verse so many times that our eyes can just skim over it, ready to move on. Let's look at it again: "I will give thanks to You, for I am fearfully and wonderfully made; wonderful are Your works, and my soul knows it very well." God is so specific, so encouraging, and so poetic. In one beautiful phrase we discover a vision for raising daughters.

Think about it. How many problems would be solved if our daughters knew they were fearfully and wonderfully made? If their *souls knew it very well*? Don't we want our daughters to embrace the truth in this Scripture, supported by powerful verses throughout the Bible that describe God's love for them and God's relationship with them?

How might this look?

Daughter's Proclamation:

I am fearfully and wonderfully made. My soul knows it well.
I am beautiful because the hands of God Almighty knit me
together in my mother's womb. I do not need to try and look like

anyone else, I do not need the attention of others to validate my beauty, and I am not desperate to fit in to any crowd. The Lord has lifted my head. I walk with confidence because I am a daughter of the King; I also walk with humility because I am a daughter of the King. I walk every day with a purpose to my life knowing that He has prepared good works in advance for me to do.

When others put me down and tell me I'm not worth anything, I take it and hand it to my heavenly Father. My Daddy tells me not to take my own revenge because vengeance is His! If you mess with me, you've messed with the wrong girl!

I can admit my faults and confess my sins because I know God is faithful and just and will forgive me and cleanse me of all unrighteousness. When trouble comes, I do not faint; I know the One who made me holds me by the hand and works all things for my good because I love Him and I am called to His purposes. I am loved; I am cherished; and I am treasured by the King of Kings! I am God's Girl![1]

How Do I Help My Daughter Know She Is God's Girl?

There is a crucial first step that lays the foundation for our parenting. For our *daughters* to know that they are God's girls, *we* must first know that they are God's girls.

Let's stop right here. Do you believe your daughter is God's girl? Do you believe the hands of the Almighty God knit her together in her mother's womb? Do you believe she is a gift from God? An arrow in your quiver? A reward?

Think about your daughter right now. Is this how you see her? We're not talking about when she was first born, all snuggly and wrapped up in a pink blanket. We're talking right now. With pigtails or braces, acne or piercings. With helping hands or hurtful words. With batting eyelashes or rolling eyes. Do you see her as God's girl?

This one point makes all the difference in how we parent and how we relate to our daughters. If I know that my daughter is a gift from God, then her newborn cries to be fed are not an interruption to my day; it is God telling me to stop my busyness and sit down and enjoy my gift.

If I know my daughter is God's girl, given to me to raise for His glory, then when I need to bring correction to her, it is with a humble heart using biblical methods. I raise God's girl in God's way.

If I know my daughter is given to me by God, I thank the Lord when she does well in school, knowing that He gave her the intelligence, and that my responsibility is to teach her to steward it for His glory.

If I know my daughter is a gift to me from *my Father* then I know that her bad attitude and disobedience can be used by Him to reveal *my own* sinful nature and conform me to the image of Jesus Christ.

If I know my daughter is created in the image of God, then when she talks back to me and argues, I speak kindly because I am talking to one that bears the imprint of God.

And when my daughter wraps her arms around me and gives me a hug, I know for sure it is a hug from God!

See the paradigm? Knowing this one truth affects everything. Let's look at two possible reactions when you lose sight of your daughter in the store:

Mom: Molly? Molly? Where are you? Come here!
Get over here right now or you'll be sorry!

Molly: Here I am...

Mom: Molly, what is wrong with you? I've told you a million times not to run away from me in the store! This is not funny, young lady. (Mom grabs child by the arm and starts dragging her to the door).

What's the message to the daughter? I've irritated Mom again.

❖

Mom: Molly? Molly? You need to come here right now!

Molly: Here I am....

Mom: Molly, hiding in those racks was disobeying Mommy. I've told you that you need to stay by me in the store. Honey, this is very important. I love you and I don't ever want to lose you!

What's the message to the daughter? I am important to Mom.

See the difference? Both reactions take the situation seriously, but the first one attacks the child, while the second one instructs and reaffirms the child.

Think how many interactions we have with our daughters each day. Each one sends a message to our daughters' hearts, and over the years, these hundreds of messages determine how our daughters see themselves, how they see God, and how they interact with us.

The Owner's Manual

Knowing that your girl is God's girl leads to a stunning directive. Remember the joking lament by many parents: "Parenting is hard. I wish this kid came with an owner's manual?" Well, when we know the truth about who actually owns our kids, then we also know this...our kids *do* come with an owner's manual: The Bible!

Because our daughters are God's girls, God's Word is then our indisputable direction on how to care for them. This is the owner's message to all of us. In this precious book we discover how much God loves us, how much we need a Savior, how to treat others, and how to live a life that brings glory to Him.

God's Word Restrains Us

We're not just talking here about the typical "parenting verses," but the entirety of Scripture! Let's face it...parenting is hard. We can get frustrated, exhausted, or irritated. In these times of temptation, the Word of God can help restrain us.

Be Gentle

In First Thessalonians 2:7, Paul is describing the care that he, Silvanus, and Timothy extended to God's people. "But we proved to be gentle among you, as a nursing mother tenderly cares for her own children." What does Paul use as a standard for care? A nursing mother! A gentle woman who tenderly cares for her own children. Mothers, does this describe us? Do we grab our children, jerking them roughly through the store, or have we taught them to be led with a gentle hand?

What about our words?

"Get away from my jewelry! I'm trying to clean.
Can't you find anything else to do than get in my way?"

Message: I am bothering Mom.

"Honey, you're not allowed to touch my jewelry. Did you want to dress up today? I'll be finished in a minute, and I'll help you get all pretty."

Message: My mom enjoys being with me.

Notice in First Thessalonians that although Paul is using a woman for the analogy, he is actually describing himself and two other *men*. Dads, are we gentle and tender with our daughters? Is our daughter regularly greeted with an affectionate hug? Do we look for ways to compliment her character and her appearance?

"Ellie, how did you miss that goal? You were kicking like an old lady!"

Message: I've disappointed my dad.

"Ellie, I'm so glad I was able to get off work early today for your game. If you want, we can practice some of those harder shots this weekend."

Message: My dad wants to help me do well.

What Should We Impart to Our Daughters? The Gospel and Our Own Lives.

See, there is so much we can get from just one verse. Let's read the next verse, First Thessalonians 2:8, through our "parenting lenses." "Having so fond an affection for you, we were well-pleased to impart to you not only the gospel of God but also our own lives, because you had become very dear to us." Isn't that a powerful description of what our parenting should look like? We should have a strong affection for our children and be well pleased to do what? Impart to them the gospel of God and our own lives.

These two directives go hand-in-hand. *To impart the gospel to our daughters, we must also impart to them our own lives.* It takes time to teach the gospel to our children. To read to them, pray with them, teach them, correct them with Scripture, encourage them with Scripture, envision them with Scripture. It takes time to work through disagreements in a God-honoring way that reflects the gospel, to confess our sins to them and ask forgiveness, to teach them to do the same.

And parents, to have the time to do all these things, we often have to say no to other pursuits that beckon to us. When we walk in the door from work, we may have to say no to the TV that's begging us to just sit and relax, and instead be dragged from room to room to hear all about the day's activities. We may have to turn off Facebook and have some face time with our daughters; be less informed on our *friends'* lives, and more informed on our daughters' lives.

Are these choices a burden to us? Well, sometimes they're difficult, but when we embrace the truth that we, like Paul, are missionaries to our children, called to disciple them daily, then we too can be "well-pleased" to pour ourselves into our daughters.

When I (Mary Lou) was about to give birth to Stephanie, an exciting opportunity arrived in the mail. My publisher was delighted with the book that I had just co-authored for pregnant women called *Expecting Joy.*[2] The envelope contained a contract and a request for a book about raising young children.

My publisher loves my book and is asking for another? That's a dream come true for any writer. But…I looked down at my ever-growing belly. There's a little life in there that would be bursting forth soon. This baby would need lots of time with me; and truthfully, I knew from experience that I needed lots of time with my baby. Time in a rocking chair may start out as a mom comforting her baby, but as the baby falls asleep, the mom gently relaxes and it is often the baby comforting the mom with his rhythmic breathing, fuzzy little head, and soothing baby smell.

I didn't want to miss this. I didn't want to rush through this season watching the clock and trying to get my baby to bed as soon as possible so I could meet my deadline. After prayer and discussion with my husband and co-author, we turned down the contract.

And I don't regret it at all. I still cherish the time I had with Stephanie and the peace I have for investing in her life. I have a wonderful relationship with my now sixteen-year-old daughter, and, as I've told her with a big smile and a hug many times, she was totally worth it.

Gentleness ≠ Anger

Let's look at another passage that is typically not quoted as a parenting verse but can encourage us in gentleness now that we see all of Scripture as our parenting guide. "For the anger of man does not achieve the righteousness of God" (James 1:20). This Scripture has been especially helpful for me (Mary Lou). I grew up as an angry young girl. I had no problem yelling at my mom, teachers, any authority. So certainly having little daughters around me would have been an easy outlet for outbursts of anger.

But I am not in the habit of yelling at my children. It is truly a miracle, and I credit it to two things: my husband's amazing example of self-control in the home, and God's power and conviction through this verse in the book of James. For I knew that if I were to yell at my children, it would be because I wanted them to obey *me*. (I certainly was not tempted to yell at them when they were just sweetly sitting and coloring.) And I also knew that if I yelled at my daughters, they would probably snap to attention quickly and hurry to obey me.

But having my children obey me is not my goal. Having daughters that love, trust, and obey God is my goal. I am ultimately after their hearts; I want them to have righteous hearts before the Lord, and this Scripture clearly teaches me that my anger will not achieve that. Yelling at my children will train them to respond to wrath, not train them to obey their God-given authorities.

In fact, a quick glance through Scripture teaches that my harsh words spoken in anger would produce the exact opposite. Proverbs 15:1 explains that a harsh word stirs up anger. So am I a fool? Do I want to stir up anger in my daughter? I don't think so! I want to be the parent that embraces the truth in the second part of that proverb: A gentle answer turns away wrath. See, the word *gentle* again. It's a strong key to effective leadership.

"Serika, what happened to your room? It's a mess!
More like a pigsty than a bedroom."

"Yeah, I got busy."

"Busy? You got busy? You know nothing about being busy. Try trading shoes with me one day. All you do is lie around and listen to music and talk on the phone. Now get up and clean this room!"

Message: Mom's on my case again. I wish she'd never come in my room.

"Serika, did you forget to clean your room?"

"Yeah, I got busy."

"I know there's a lot going on right now. Did something else come up?"

"Yeah, I got a lot of phone calls."

"Well, Honey, I understand that your friends want to talk to you. You are such a great friend and you give great advice. But when I ask you to clean your room, I expect you to remember to do it. Maybe you could have just straightened up while you talked on the phone."

Message: Mom tries to understand the things that are important to me.

While we are on the topic of anger and harshness, here are a few crucial comments: Fellow parents, our words are loud, even when our volume is not. Think about the adults you know. Does anyone really struggle with "I remember that lady down the street that didn't like my dress?" No, it is not usually the remarks from friends or strangers that shape us; it is the words of our parents.

So many adults today are tortured and weighed down by the words their parents spoke over them:

"You can't do anything right."

"What is wrong with you? Are you stupid?"

"You ruin everything."

"Too bad you're not pretty like your sister."

"Get out of my face. I never want to see you again."

Painful Memories

As you read this, are you reminded of painful words from your own childhood? Don't stuff these in the back of your mind anymore where you're doomed to hear echoes of these attacks. Bring them to the Lord who "binds up the broken-hearted" (Isa. 61:1). You heard these painful words as a child; now look at them with the maturity of an adult and realize this: *These words should not have been said to me or about me. I do not know or understand all the things going on in my parents' lives at that time, but they were wrong for treating me this way. And today, and every time these verbal arrows come my way, I choose to forgive my parents.*

Go back to Psalm 139:14 in the beginning of this chapter and read it for yourself. *You* are fearfully and wonderfully made. Read the Daughter's Proclamation and claim these verses for yourself—these powerful truths from Scripture can heal a man's heart, too. As you throw out all the negative things that were said about you, immerse yourself in the truth from God about who you really are. This truth can set you free!

Knowing the power of a parent's words, it is imperative that we choose our words and attitudes carefully, bearing in mind again that we are caring for God's girl and that we will be accountable to Him. Jesus tells us in Matthew 12:36 that we will be accountable for every word that comes out of our mouth and Matthew 25:40 tells us that whatever we do to the least of these we've done unto Him. We've been clearly warned!

Are You Struggling with Anger?

Fellow parents, are you struggling? If you have already set a tone of anger in your home, here's what to do: Repent! Read verses on anger, outbursts of anger, and the hot-tempered man.[3] Ask the Holy Spirit to bring conviction and repent. Repent to the Lord, your spouse, and your daughter. Pray before heading into a difficult situation, pray during a situation, ask for input from others after a situation.

There have been seasons when the struggles with my daughter seemed endless and I (Mary Lou) just wanted to scream. I would often go back in our bedroom and say over and over to myself, "The anger of man does not produce the righteousness of God. The anger of man does not produce the righteousness of God" until my heart calmed down. Also, because I live in a fishbowl (people are around me all the time), I would often ask my husband or children for input and observations on how I handled a situation.

We must remember that avoiding anger in our interactions with our daughters does not guarantee they will have good attitudes. But we are parenting for the Lord and leaving the results up to Him.

One more thought. If you grew up in an angry home, you may be tempted to think that you have no choice. That's how your parents were, that's all you know, and that's how you'll always be. No, no, no! Resist that lie! Did you like being yelled at? Did you like cowering in the corner while your parent went on a verbal tirade? Did you like the fear of wondering when the next outburst of anger would come? No! Use your painful memories to increase your commitment to never again, by the grace of God, make your daughter feel that way. *Let your childhood suffering turn into a parenting triumph.* The grace of God can do this in you and through you.

(Note: Stormie Omartian's biography may be helpful here. It's simply called *Stormie: A Story of Forgiveness and Healing*.[4] It is her account of the abuses against her, her own sins, and God's amazing power to forgive and enable us to forgive others. Her follow-up book, *Lord, I Want to be Whole*[5], gives a detailed, behind-the-scenes look at how Stormie prayed and fought through difficulties and made the long and often difficult journey to victorious and fruitful living.)

Be Genuine

So as we've seen, we must be gentle when raising our daughters. We also must be genuine. What is the main complaint against Christians? We're hypocrites. And what's the main complaint of young girls from Christian homes? Sadly, the same thing.

I (Mary Lou) was talking with a young adult who was struggling through some difficult issues. "Your parents are Christians," I responded. "Have you talked to them to get their thoughts?"

Her response was direct, and all too common, "No, I don't want anything to do with the type of Christians they are."

First of all, sometimes a daughter can just be upset because she doesn't like the truly biblical standards that are upheld in her home. If that's the case, as parents we can seek counsel from other trusted and fruitful leaders, and if our parenting lines up with God's Word, we need to stand firm.

"Dad, my alarm didn't go off this morning and I missed first period. Can you write a note for me?"

"What would you like me to say?"

"That I was at an orthodontist appointment or something. I had a test in that class and without an excuse I'll get an 'F'."

"I can't lie for you."

"Well, it's not really lying. It wouldn't be fair for me to get the 'F.' I really know the material. I could take the test now and get an 'A.' I just need an excuse so I can take a make-up test this afternoon."

"Just tell your teacher your alarm didn't go off."

"Yeah, right! We're wasting time here. Just write something so I can get going."

"Honey, I understand what you're saying, but I'm just not going to lie for you."

"But I'll get an 'F.' Is that what you really want?"

"No, it's not what I really want. You know I want you to do well in school. But I am not going to disobey God, which is exactly what you are asking me to do. I will call your teacher, tell her your alarm didn't go off, and I will leave work early to pick you up from a make-up test, but I will not lie. I want our home, and you, to be blessed, and having a father who compromises will not benefit you in the long run. I love you and want you to know that I am a man of my word, even when it's difficult."

"Augh! You drive me crazy."

*Message now: My dad won't lie for me. Message later:
I can trust my dad to tell me the truth.*

If our daughters are upset at us for holding to clear biblical principles like the above scenario, then we can confidently trust God that He will bring good fruit from this (Isa. 55:11).

Sometimes though, a daughter's struggle with her parents' Christianity stems from her parents' hypocrisy. We must be genuine with our daughters. Having Christian parents should be an advantage in our shaky world. Should give our daughters a profound sense of being cherished. Should give our daughters an excitement to bring friends home. Should give our daughters a confidence that they can get wisdom from their parents. Should give our daughters the security of being forgiven, the hope of change, and the comfort of being loved through it all.

Genuine = Honest

What does it mean to be genuine in our parenting? It means to be honest about the truths in Scripture and about the truths in our lives.

"Honey, would you please forgive me? Mommy was angry and I shouldn't have yelled at you. I was wrong."

Message: Mommy sins too! And she asks for forgiveness.

"Bianca, I want to ask your forgiveness. God showed me that when we were talking earlier, I wasn't being compassionate. I knew you were having a hard day, and I just wanted to get things done. I'm truly sorry."

Message: Dad listens to God in raising me.

In our family, our children know our struggles with sin. To the degree that it is appropriate, we try to live open lives with them, and we expect the same from them. They all have heard detailed stories of Mom's battle with pride and seen her tears of thankfulness as she shared God's power for great change in her life. Dad has confessed to the children many times of being thoughtless to Mom (after confessing to her) and has asked the children for forgiveness many times when he has been distracted or having a bad attitude.

Our children are aware that we don't keep soda in the house because Mom was addicted to it, that Dad looks away from immodest billboards or movie scenes, and that Mom and Dad pray about decisions. They know Dad gets up early in the morning to pray, and they have seen Mom crying in prayer in her room many times, especially during difficult seasons.

Our children know we don't always agree with each other, but we work things out in a biblical way.

"I know, Silvia, that it's hard to obey."

"But Dad is wrong!"

"I know you think that. But Ephesians 6:1 makes it clear: 'Children, obey your parents in the Lord, for this is right.' He's not asking you to sin. You don't have to agree with Dad, but you do need to obey him."

"You just don't understand!"

"Oh, yes I do! Do you think I agree with every decision Dad makes? No, of course not. I share my thoughts with Dad, but sometimes he just makes a decision I think is wrong. What do I do? Well, I trust God to work through Dad. I try to keep my conscience clean and I trust God to use the situation for my good" (Rom. 8:28).

Message: My mom also has to do things she doesn't want to do, and she trusts God through it.

All our children can tell you the story of when Dad brought the dog home…the story of Second Chance. Rich had been driving home and saw a lost Chihuahua running down the road. He got out of his car and called to the dog. Just at that moment another car screeched to a halt, nearly running over the dog. The little dog leapt into my husband's arms. Rich was delighted and instantly called him Second Chance. When he saw the dog had no collar and couldn't find any neighbors to claim the dog, he brought him home for the night until he could find the dog's owner.

The children were thrilled; Mom was not. I am not a big fan of pets, and I did not want this dog in my home, even for one night. While the kids were running all around with the dog, squealing with joy and taking lots of pictures, I was fuming in the corner. *How could Rich bring a dog into this house? He knows I wouldn't like this at all. He is being so selfish.*

"Mom," the children kept calling out, "come and play with Second Chance." But I refused and scowled at everyone. The children just don't understand, I reasoned. This is a marital issue. My husband has purposely done something he knows will bother me.

The next day, the owner was found and Rich returned the dog. The children continued to question my reaction, but I emphatically explained that I just don't like dogs.

A few weeks later, Rich and I were driving home from a weekly Bible study with some of our children. Because we include our children in Bible studies and Sunday morning messages, we are able to have great discussions about what we are all learning together and how it applies to each of our lives. We were talking about the exhortations in Scripture against grumbling, and I was strongly echoing what was taught that night— specifically for the benefit of certain children in the car that I felt needed the timely reminder.

Our oldest daughter piped up, "You didn't have a good attitude when Dad brought home that dog." There was a chorus through the car of "uh-huhs" and vigorous nodding of the heads. "Mom, your attitude was terrible. You were pouting just because you didn't like what Dad had done. That's what you always tell us not to do."

I responded with a few pitiful "you don't understand" comments, but the correction stuck with me. As I prayed about it that night, the Lord convicted me. I was grumbling and complaining and being a terrible example for my children. After asking the Lord to forgive me, I went to all my family members, confessed my sin, and asked their forgiveness.

I'm thankful for Second Chance because that dog exposed my heart and helped remove some hypocrisy from it. Primarily, I'm thankful for second chances…that God forgives me and gives me new opportunities for victories where I have previously failed.

This is how genuineness looks in our home. It will look different in yours, but it's really just honestly seeking to grow in the Lord, overcome our sins, and love others in a transparent manner that encourages, equips, and envisions our children and others who visit our home.

God's Word Revives Us

Holding the entire Word of God as our parenting manual not only **restrains** us but also **revives** us! Let's be honest—raising daughters is exhausting. Physically exhausting when they're little and emotionally exhausting when they're older. And if you happen to have older children and younger children, then expect to be up early running around and up late talking. It is totally worth it and totally rewarding, but what do we do when we are smack dab in the middle of the confusion and exhaustion and the rewards seem way off in the dim future? We pray and cling to God and His Word!

Notice the word *cling*. This is not a quick prayer offered up and a glance through Scripture. This is a desperate grasp by a drowning parent holding on to the rock of hope. It can look different in each season of life, but dependence on God is essential.

The Least of These

Early one morning, Rich had already left for work and the sun was just breaking through the blinds. The children were all asleep, and I was snuggled in my comfy bed, so excited to rest my worn-out body. Then I heard it…rustling in the bassinet next to me. I held my breath. *Oh, please God, let her go back to sleep. I am so tired.* The rustling increased and then I heard her. Just a grunt at first, then faint cries, progressing louder and louder. I squeezed my eyes shut. No, it's way too early. It felt like I just put the baby to bed. I was drained and delirious from being up night after night and then caring for my other children during the day.

At that moment, I would have literally paid someone $1,000 to get my daughter up and change her diaper and bring her to me.

Well, no one came, so I rolled out of bed and started my day. As I was standing at the changing table putting a new diaper on my daughter, a voice spoke to me through the fog. I felt the Lord encourage me, "Whatever you do to the least of these you've done unto me."[6]

What? I've heard this verse many times and it always involved images of a woman like Mother Teresa feeding the poor in India or a man like Jim

Elliot looking for creative ways to share God's love with the natives in Ecuador. As I stood there, disheveled in my little bedroom in my little home in my little town, I suddenly knew this: I am serving the Lord! And from that point on, I would regularly speak to myself throughout the following days and years: I am changing diapers for Jesus!

Parenting Olympics

See, our lives would be so much easier if parenting got the honor that the Olympics do. Can't you just hear the announcer:

Bob is driving home from a long day at the office. He glances down at his gauges and sees the needle close to 'E'. As he pulls into the gas station, a text comes in from his wife: pick up diapers, please. Diapers or gas? How shall he spend the last $20 in his wallet? He hesitates, then runs in and returns with a package victoriously in his arm.

He hurries home, trying to outrun the remaining gas fumes and planning to rummage through his drawer for gas money later on that night. He pulls in the driveway and suddenly faces a daunting obstacle course. Look at him go, folks. He steps over bikes, effortlessly picks up a toppled doll stroller, and with vision that few men possess, sees the play dough on the step and avoids it. This man is amazing! But his challenges have just begun. What will he find when he opens the door? His keen ear has already discerned whining and a banging of pots and pans. Slowly he turns the handle and pushes open the door.

The onslaught is intense. "Daddy, Daddy, you're home!" Little peanut-butter-covered hands grab his wool suit. His face grimaces, but look at that self-control. He quickly smiles and picks up his little girl.

"Hi, Sweetie." He gives her a big hug (oooh, bonus points here) and sets her back down. He looks for his wife,

gives her a kiss (more bonus points), and quickly heads for the couch.

"Honey," his wife calls out, "could you help Savannah with her volcano project and hold the baby? I need to start dinner."

He stops midstride and the crowd goes silent. How will he respond to this change of course? He looks at the couch, he looks at the remote, he looks at his wife. This man studied at the school of biblical truths. He is a top student, memorizing and teaching classes throughout the city. But is he prepared for this?

He strides over to his wife, takes the baby from her arms, reaches down, takes his daughter's hand, and says with a grin, "Come on, Savannah. I've been wanting to blow something up all day, but my boss wouldn't let me!"

The crowd grows wild and the judges unanimously hold up large number ten scorecards.

We would parent so much better if we had this daily moment-by-moment encouragement. That's why it's important to know the truth because it is not often what we see or hear. For the Word of God explains to us that we are actually in a type of Olympics and there is a great crowd watching us. Not only our spouse, children, and friends, but also a heavenly crowd of witnesses.

Hebrews 12:1 encourages us, "Therefore, since we have so great a cloud of witnesses surrounding us, let us also lay aside every encumbrance and the sin which so easily entangles us, and let us run with endurance the race that is set before us." How cool is that? A crowd of heavenly hosts cheering us on.

Oh, to be like Elisha's servant who was fearful of the enemies surrounding him. Ever feel that way? Fearful? Overwhelmed? Surrounded? For just a moment, the Lord opened the eyes of Elisha's servant beyond their limited earthly abilities, and what did he see? He was surrounded by flaming chariots fighting for him (2 Kings 6:16-17). As children of God, this is true for us too. Oh, may we get a glimpse!

Let's fill our hearts and minds with truth. Colossians 3:23-24 says, "Whatever you do, do your work heartily, as for the Lord rather than for men, knowing that from the Lord you will receive the reward of the inheritance. It is the Lord Christ whom you serve." Wow!

Is parenting work? Most definitely.

How are we to parent? Heartily.

For whom? The Lord.

Knowing what? That from the Lord we will receive a reward.

How awesome is that? We may not be exactly sure what that reward will be, but we know it will be from God and therefore it'll be way better than the man-made medals awarded at the Olympics.

You Are a Hero

Do you like to hear stories of heroic missionaries that trample over obstacles to bring the good news to sinners? Well, that's you! You are trampling over the obstacles of deception and worldliness surrounding your daughter to bring her the truth of God's love. You are pushing through the darkness of confusion and a lack of moral standards to bring her the light of God's Word. You are fighting against media moguls who tell your daughter she must starve herself to look like the airbrushed model on the cover of the latest magazine, and instead you are bringing her the satisfying Bread of Life. You are breaking through the culture that expects teens to be selfish and depressed, and bringing your daughter the refreshment of a life lived with purpose for the King Almighty. You are a hero! You are a missionary! And you are discipling an eternal soul for the glory of God. Is it difficult? Of course it is. Anything of this magnitude is bound to be fraught with obstacles.

Do you love God? Do you love your daughter? Jesus' words are clear to each of us: "Greater love has no one than this, that one lay down his life for his friends" (John 15:13). We have a mission. We are running the race with a glorious crowd of witnesses, knowing there is a reward at the end, and often many rewards along the way. *The days are long, but the years are short*. Let's throw off the sin that so easily entangles us and run the race that's been set before us: raising our daughters to love, trust, and obey God…raising them to know that they are God's Girls!

Prayer

> *Lord, help me to see that my daughter is a gift from You and that she is fearfully and wonderfully made. May the truth of Scripture be the guide to all my parenting. May it restrain me from speaking destructive words to my daughter and revive me when I am weary.*

[1] Psalm 139:13-14; Deuteronomy 26:18; Isaiah 52:7; Psalm 3:3; Ephesians 3:12; 2 Corinthians 5:20; James 4:10; Jeremiah 29:11; Ephesians 2:10; 1 Peter 5:7; Romans 12:19; 1 John 1:9; Isaiah 40:31; Isaiah 41:13; Romans 8:28; 1 John 4:19; Ephesians 5:29; Psalm 16:9.

[2] Mary Lou Graham and Marianne Kelso, *Expecting Joy* (San Diego: Legacy Press, 1998).

[3] Proverbs 15:1 & 18; Proverbs 22:24-25; Galatians 5:19-21; Ephesians 4:31; James 1:19-20.

[4] Stormie Omartian, Stormie: *A Story of Forgiveness and Healing* (Eugene, OR: Harvest House Publishers, 1986).

[5] Stormie Omartian, *Lord, I Want to Be Whole* (Nashville: Thomas Nelson, Inc., 2000).

[6] Matthew 25:40.

The Daughters Speak

Stephanie Says...

It's not uncommon for me to be walking around with my shoulders hunched and Mom to whisper, "You're God's girl," reminding me to stand up straight and tall. My parents have consistently demonstrated to me by their words and actions that I am a gift from God, and they are raising me to follow His calling on my life.

As you were reading this chapter, did you notice that it was less about actions and more about the heart? That has been taught to me my entire life! Any time that I have a struggle, my mom doesn't just say, "You need to stop doing XYZ," rather she asks, "Honey, why is it that you did XYZ?" and a lot of other questions until she gets to the heart of the matter. Then my motive is addressed and worked through. I know that my parent's correction is meant to build me up in Christ, not tear me down.

The other night, my parents asked each of us children if we knew that they were for us and wanted us to succeed in life. "Yes!" I replied with confidence. I am their "puppy dog daughter" as Dad calls me. Basically, I am constantly jumping from idea to idea, starting many things and finishing...a few. But again and again as I ask, "Can I do this?" or, "Can we do that?" I never hear frustration coming from my parents. Rather, they listen, see where I can implement a particular idea, and then support me as I do it. Yes, I know my parents are for me!

Mom regularly checks my heart
And Daddy guards it, too
In life they've given me a start
And shown me what to do

From changing diapers and giving bottles
To late night talks and advice
Their lives have always been awesome models
Of people who live for Christ

They're for me, I know it well
My soul knows it too
"I'm God's girl" they happily tell
And God, I'll live for You!

Dads: Do not skip this chapter! There is much here that can encourage you in how you interact with your daughter. Also, your understanding of the mother/ daughter relationship will be crucial as you protect and guide these two women that you love.

2

Like Mother, Like Daughter

Encouraging and Enjoying Your Daughter

Let me say this upfront: I don't want to be my daughter's best friend.

What? You don't want to laugh with her, hang out with her, talk with her, cry with her? Isn't that the goal of motherhood? Isn't that what good mothers do?

Oh, I do all these things with my daughters. A glimpse through my life over the years would find me rocking my daughter, crawling on the floor playing horsey, putting dresses on Barbies, and bows in hair. You could catch me playing games with my daughters, watching movies, listening to seminars, and learning new dances. You may find me praying with my daughters, crying with my daughters, worshipping with my daughters, bringing advice to my daughters, and receiving advice from my daughters. I have great relationships with all four of my daughters. Each of them live for the Lord, and we serve the Lord together regularly.

But I do not want to be my daughter's best friend for this simple reason: it would be a demotion!

For you see, I am called to be all those things that define a best friend... and more! My relationships with my daughters are not "fair" relationships. They are not built on equality and an even exchange of give and take. Yes,

I learn much from my daughters and get immeasurable pleasure from my times with them, but let's be honest. Looking over the landscape of our lives, I primarily give to them…and they take…and that's ok.

Moms, let's stop for a moment. Are you ok with this? Are you ok having an "unfair" relationship with your daughter? Are you ok extending more service, more grace, more understanding, more patience, more hours of listening, more expressions of love? Or do you expect equal treatment from your daughter? Do you expect her to treat you the way you treat her? Are you expecting her to fill some empty places in your heart? Are you regularly aware of, and even quick to mention, how much you do and how little she does? Is this a biblical perspective?

Deuteronomy 6:6-7 draws an inspiring picture of the parent/child relationship: "These words, which I am commanding you today, shall be on your heart; and you shall teach them diligently to your sons (*daughters*) and shall talk of them when you sit in your house and when you walk by the way and when you lie down and when you rise up." Two things leap off the page to me. First, we are to be teaching and encouraging our daughters in the Lord…constantly. As we walk, as we lie down, as we sit, basically in all situations. Second, we are to be with our daughters, sharing life with them, enjoying them.

Encouraging and Enjoying! That's our role; that's our privilege. Knowing this, and walking in this, will bring a great peace and joy to our hearts.

What Keeps Us From Being Encouraging?

Most of us have this vision for our relationships with our daughters. But somehow, along the way, we often take a wrong turn. Sometimes we suddenly wake up and find that we are not on the road we started on.

Though each mother/daughter relationship is unique and formed by our personalities, sin patterns, relationships with the Lord, experiences, and family dynamics, there are several common temptations for moms that lure us into stumbling onto the wrong path.

Not Understanding Our Role

As moms, we are called to be the more mature woman. You've heard the saying: "God loves us right where we are; but He loves us too much to leave us there." God loved us while we were still sinners, yet He is conforming us to the image of His Son, Jesus Christ (John 3:16 & Romans 8:29). We need to model God's love for our daughters: accept them where they are and help them to grow.

The truth is, I am not always more mature than my daughters. They are more mature than me in many areas, and I am regularly inspired by their lives. But I am called to the *role* of the more mature one. It is a positional calling, whether I am there emotionally or not, I must fulfill this role.

For example, let's take the area of confidence. All of my daughters are way more confident than I am. But I've been used by the Lord to build their confidence in many ways (along with the strong support of my husband and other leaders). I speak truth to my daughters. I tell them they are beautiful. I compliment them specifically. I honor them to others. I regularly draw upon their giftings; make sure they feel needed. I tell them they are worth protecting, their hearts are highly valuable, and their specific strengths are given to them by God because of the unique call they have on their lives. All of these things are true; I say them all the time and desire to treat my daughters accordingly.

Many times, I know God is speaking to me through my own words. My daughters embrace these truths quicker than I do; their hearts are more fertile, less scarred than mine. So although I don't walk fully in these truths of Scripture, I can confidently speak them to my daughters because my confidence does not lie in my experiences, but in the inerrant word of the Lord. And it is my *role*, my calling, to speak these encouraging truths to my daughters, and along the way, I grow too.

This is a role that we must intentionally embrace, or we may create an unhealthy dynamic in our home. How might this look?

Mom: Toshiko, why didn't you do these dishes?
I told you to do them before I got home.

Toshiko: Oh, yeah. I forgot.

Mom: You forgot? You forgot! I've been busy all day running all over town and I ask you to do one thing, just one thing! You don't care a thing about me and how hard I work. You only care about yourself!

Message to Toshiko: Mom is freaking out again!

What's wrong with this scenario? Well, one thing is that the mother has not embraced her position. She has spent the day serving others and may be possibly struggling with bitterness. Is it a bad thing to be busy during the day? Is it a bad thing to be serving others? Should Toshiko be made to feel guilty for her mom's day? If Mom is not feeling the pleasure of the Lord for laying down her life and serving others, is that Toshiko's fault?

What is the real issue here? The real issue is that Toshiko did not do what was asked. It's that simple and that is what should simply be addressed. This requires more maturity; a mom that is not led by her emotions, or, at least, a woman who takes a deep breath, offers up a silent request to her Father, and attempts to embrace her responsibility to train her daughter with gentleness.

Mom: Toshiko, why didn't you do the dishes like I asked?

Toshiko: Oh, yeah. I forgot.

Mom: Toshiko, we are a family, and it's important that we each do our part to keep our home running well. When I ask you to do something, I need to be able to trust that you will do it. Clean up the kitchen now and please put away these groceries too when you're done.

Message: Mom wants me to do what she asks.

If Toshiko's mom is not feeling valued for the way she serves her family, she first needs to take it to the Lord. Colossians 3:23-24 encourages us to work heartedly at whatever task our hand finds, knowing that it is the Lord God we're serving, who sees us and will reward us! Hallelujah! Yes, we need to teach our daughters to be thankful, but throwing a blanket of guilt on them will not accomplish this.

Dads, this is a way that you can help your wife and daughter. You can cultivate an attitude of gratitude for your wife. The way you speak to your wife, and about your wife, is powerful. Do you thank your wife often for the ways she serves? Do you vocalize specific appreciation for her talents and giftings? Does your daughter know you think her mother is amazing, better than you deserve, and worthy of honor? Are you publically and privately drawing your daughter's attention to her mother's outward and inner beauty?

Suffocating Our Daughter with a Heavy Blanket of Worldly Guilt

Let's look back at the topic of guilt. This is a common tool used by moms, and put in our hands by the enemy...our daughter's enemy and our enemy. For when this tool is wielded, everyone is hurt.

My husband, daughter, and I went in to see our pastor for help in walking through a difficult season. As he was listening to us and praying for us, our pastor remarked to me that I carried a lot of guilt. "Oh, no, I don't," I responded. "Quite the opposite. I struggle with pride." My pastor smiled at me and encouraged me to get a notebook and write down every time I feel guilty.

Second Corinthians 7:9-11 is a clear description of the crucial difference between guilt and godly sorrow. To be convicted of a sin, to feel the weight of your wrong, is a beautiful thing...because of what it leads to:

I now rejoice, not that you were made sorrowful, but that you were made sorrowful to the point of repentance; for you were made sorrowful according to the will of God, so that you might not suffer loss in anything through us. For the sorrow that is according to the will of God produces a repentance without regret, leading to salvation, but the sorrow of the world produces death. For behold what earnestness this very thing, this godly sorrow, has produced in you: what vindication of yourselves, what indignation, what fear, what longing, what zeal, what avenging of wrong! In everything you demonstrated yourselves to be innocent in the matter.

When we disobey God, we should feel terrible, like a weight is pressing on us (Psalm 38). This feeling, caused by God's discipline for our sin, will leave us with godly sorrow, which leads to a desire to repent, walk in the Lord's cleansing forgiveness, and an urgency to repair the damage in whatever way we can.

Worldly guilt is not like that. It is feeling despair for something that may or may not be sin, and it leads to death, usually a death in our spirit.

So, I did what my pastor suggested. I was shocked! I felt guilt all the time! When I told my daughters about this, they were not surprised. They had already seen this in me, yet didn't quite know how to express it. They shared other examples of where they had seen me walking in guilt, hesitating and questioning myself. My list grew and grew, and I learned, when the weight hits me, to stop, pray, and ask God to show me if I have sinned and need to repent or if I am feeling worldly guilt again.

Even as I sat down at my local bagel shop to write this chapter, the guilty thoughts rolled over me: *I should've returned that DVD in the mail today because the kids are waiting for the next one to arrive. I should have thrown a load of dark clothing in the wash before I left. My cell is ringing. It's one of my daughter's friends. I should answer it, but I need to work on this book. I'm taking up a whole booth with my computer and books. Maybe I should move? Will the workers here be irritated with me sitting here all afternoon?* Oh, the thoughts kept coming and coming and I kept praying and praying my way through.

Why do I struggle with guilt? One of the reasons is that I am an only child, and I was raised by a single mother. If my mom was upset, whose fault was it? *Obviously mine,* I thought as a child. *Who else could be blamed?* And so I carried this pattern of guilt through my young life into adulthood.

Most women I talk to, though, struggle with guilt. This is important to recognize and overcome for our relationship with God, but it's also important to be aware of so that we don't throw worldly guilt on our daughters. When I was in college I volunteered at a crisis pregnancy center. The number one reason girls gave for wanting to abort their babies was because they didn't want to tell their mothers – they didn't want to disappoint them, so they got the abortions without their mothers knowing it. Now, when we do pro-life work, it is often the mothers bringing their daughters in for an abortion. The daughters we talk to still fear disappointing their mothers, but this time their mothers want them to finish school and a baby would interfere with that goal. A new age; but a familiar motherly guilt.

How do we know if we are suffocating our daughters with a blanket of worldly guilt? One way is to examine if we are overreacting to situations. Do our daughters color out of the lines, make a mess when they cook, spend hours singing in their rooms, paint their nails in crazy designs? Do these things matter? How do we react? Do our daughters want to wear a braid on one side, paint their rooms purple with yellow polka dots, and plant okra in the backyard? That's probably ok.

One of the best words I've said to my daughters is "Sure." *Mom, can we make mud pies?* Sure! *Can you make popcorn and watch a movie with me?* Sure! *Mom, can I practice braiding your hair?* Sure! *Can I cut my Barbie's hair?* Sure! *Can I bring a friend home for dinner?* Sure! *Can I start a Bible Club with my little brothers and sisters?* Sure! *Can I teach a ballet class?* Sure! *Can I volunteer at the church office?* Sure!

Yes, as a mom we look for patterns in our daughters' lives and we watch their actions closely because we know according to Luke 6:45-49 that our actions and words reveal our hearts, and what is in our hearts is most important. But so many of the things our daughters want to do are just ways of expressing their unique personality from God, which, as shocking as this may be, is probably different from ours!

And this is where it gets dangerous. So often, as moms, we are tempted to bring correction to our daughters for things we don't *like*.

Treating Preferences as Sin

Stop right here. Don't rush past this point. Let's examine it closely. For this is another temptation along the way that can trip us and send us into a pretty deep pit. If we bring correction to our daughters for areas based solely on our personal preferences, they have no way to biblically process it. They are just left with one thing: the weight of worldly guilt.

"Correction" from a mom can come in many forms. Correction is not only a response as described in the clear teachings of Scripture on how we are to discipline our children. Our daughters can feel "corrected" from our complaining, sighing, or rolling of the eyes.

Oh, wait. Does this sound familiar – complaining, sighing, rolling the eyes? Yes, we too can be tempted to have the exact same immature responses that our daughters do, and then wonder why our daughters act that way. Remember the beginning of this chapter. We must walk in our *position* as a mother; we do not have the freedom to react like our daughters.

What do we get upset about? What matters to us? That our daughters are "safe" and living at home? That they have the hair color we want, are the weight we think is appropriate, listen to the style of music we like, have the same hobbies we do? When we have a negative reaction in these areas of "preferences", it only produces worldly guilt in our daughters: *Mom doesn't like this.* Instead of biblical conviction: *This is displeasing to God, and I need His help to change.*

The very serious danger here is this: *If we react strongly to things just because we don't like them, then when we need to bring our daughters correction on truly biblical issues, they won't know the difference.* And when mom's preferences blend with God's commands, daughters will often reject the whole package! Sadly, this happens so often to girls that grew up in Christian homes.

Fear Stifles Encouragement

As I look back on over two decades of raising daughters, there is one thing that has consistently damaged my mothering and kept me from giving them the encouragement they needed. When I look at situations or seasons that I did not handle well, I can see one thing rising to the top: Fear.

Fear of harm. Fear of failure. Fear of man.

Fear of Harm

I had taken my children out running errands all morning and visiting the library. I was exhausted and just wanted to get home, put the little ones to bed for naptime, and have my quiet time with the Lord.

So when we got home and tumbled out of the van, I rushed around getting everyone to bed. Finally everyone was settled and I headed to my room, but wait! I didn't see Becky. She was old enough that she didn't need naps, but I didn't remember seeing her anywhere. I called out and looked through the house. Nowhere! I ran around asking the children. No, they didn't know where she was. I grabbed the keys and went running out to the van. I flung the door open and there she stood. In the back of the van, leaning over, holding her library books, sweating from the heat.

"Becky, what are you doing?" I cried out.

"Everyone shut the door when they got out and I couldn't open it because my arms were filled with books."

I stared at her, stunned. "Why didn't you put your books down and open the door?" I exclaimed.

"I don't know," was her reply.

I was furious! How could she not know to put down her books? She could have passed out! What if I hadn't noticed she was missing! I brought her inside, gave her water, and barraged her with a ceaseless flow of words explaining the dangers of her decision.

Years later, the Lord brought this incident back to my mind. He had been challenging me on having compassion for Becky when she struggled in ways that I didn't understand: in school, in organizing, in life. As I reflected on that day when she was "stuck" in the van, God showed me that fear had driven my response. And my fear had blinded me to what should have also arisen in this situation: compassion. Why didn't Becky put down her books? What was in her, or not in her, that kept her from making that logical decision? I brought this up to Becky, which she remembered well, and I apologized for a lack of compassion, driven by fear.

Fear of Failure

Becky reminded me of another time fear had kept me from responding well. (Thank God for open communication and lots of accountability.) Our living situation had recently changed, and Becky was struggling greatly with the adjustment. I found a note she had scribbled which read, *I've got to get out of here.*

What? First, shock rose up in me. We love our daughter. She's being raised by two parents in a Christian home. We actively apply God's love and God's Word in our lives. How can she want to leave? (This was just one of many things that surprised me about raising children: though we submit our parenting to the Lord and diligently apply His truths and repent when we fail, our children may still have serious struggles. This honestly surprised me. I share it here, hoping to help younger moms.)

The second feeling was fear. Get out of here? Is she thinking about running away? Where did that idea come from? I mentally ran through the movies we'd watched. No. The friends she had. No.

I went to Becky with the note. I explained all the dangers involved with running away and what could happen to little girls out there. We talked on and on...actually I talked on and on and she listened.

I was afraid. Afraid she might actually sneak out one night. And my fear was so large that I didn't ask the obvious question: *Why do you feel like you've got to get out of here?* Just that one question, and an open, listening heart, would have helped Becky greatly. But fear blinded me to the real issue and the true cry of her heart. I John 4:18 says, "There is no fear in love, but perfect love casts out fear." My fear limited my ability to give Becky the encouragement and love she needed.

Fear of Man

Another fear that can be a stumbling block for us is the fear of man. Worrying about what others think of us, our daughters, our families. Again, the Word of God is filled with wisdom for all of our parenting dilemmas: Fear of man will prove to be a snare (Prov. 29:25).

On the one hand, our reputation does matter. We are to reflect well on Christ. According to 2 Corinthians 3:2-3 we are living letters, examples to the world of Christ, salvation, and love. Truthfully, just having a Christian bumper sticker can make us better drivers because we are a walking (and driving) testimony to the entire world. We want to look out for the interests of others (Philippians 2:4), and be at peace with all men as far as it is up to us (Romans 12:18). We want to be teachable, receiving correction and observations from others graciously. To do all of this, we must be aware of the thoughts and concerns of others. But this is not the same thing as fear.

We have fear of man when a man's standards direct us instead of the Lord's standards. Here are some examples:

How do we respond when our daughters disobey at a birthday party? Are we embarrassed? Do we try to ignore them or hush them up real quick and hope that nobody saw? Or do we swing the other way and correct them more sternly when we are in a Christian crowd, while at home we would honestly let them get away with it?

Is there one woman's opinion that matters the most to us? Do her compliments carry us through the day, or her criticisms cause us to scurry and enforce instant change in our parenting?

Are we setting standards in our home, obedience charts, household rules, clothing guidelines, etc, based on what another family does? Do we implement rules in our home solely because a "good parenting book" recommended them without praying, searching the Scriptures, or checking with our husbands first? Fear of man, expressed by letting man's word or opinions direct our parenting choices, will prove to be a snare for both us and our children.

Jealousy

How can we know if we struggle with jealousy? Are we jealous of other moms, other families, other daughters? Do we compare our daughters to others and wish ours were different? Moms, let us not be deceived here. Our daughters can sense this. Just like we want them to "feel" our love, they will "feel" this comparison. Do we ridicule other families to make ourselves feel better? *Well, of course the Petersons are at a Bible seminar this weekend while we're standing in line for the Star Wars movie. Oh boy, what a "fun" time for them!* Or do we intentionally honor godliness in other families? *The Petersons are at a Bible seminar? I love the way they devote themselves to the Word of God!*

Or how about jealousy toward our own daughters? This can be a hard one to identify because almost any mom would deny this immediately; it sounds so wrong. Jealousy towards our daughters can be rooted in the first point we discussed in this chapter...a lack of understanding our role. We are not in competition with our daughters. We are called to be their biggest cheerleaders. We are to help them to be all God's called them to be, rejoice in their successes, and help them through their failures. Like we saw from Deuteronomy 6, we are to encourage them along the way, at all times.

Are we jealous of their beauty and youth, insulting them to make ourselves feel better? *Let's measure your waist. Oh, my waist was 5 inches smaller when I was your age.* Are we resentful of their friends, jealous of the time she spends with them?

When Marilyn came home for her summer break from college,
she mentioned to her mom that she was going to the
beach that Saturday with some friends.

Her mom's face contorted, "But I had planned on
us going shopping this weekend."

"I didn't know," Marilyn responded. "You should have asked me."

"I don't need to ask you. You're my daughter! Obviously you don't
want to spend time with me," the mother yelled and walked away.

Message to daughter: I am a terrible daughter, and I've upset my mother.

This could easily be avoided.

Marilyn: Hey Mom I'm going to the beach this
Saturday with some friends.

Mom: Oh, I was hoping we could go shopping. Who are you going with?

Marilyn: Allie and Belinda are picking me up at 8.

Mom: Well, the weather is supposed to be perfect for the beach.
Want to go shopping during the week?
There's a new store that just opened, and I think you'll love it.

Message: Mom wants to hang out with me.

How Does Jealousy Affect Our Parenting?

James 3:13-17 says:

Who among you is wise and understanding? Let him show by his good behavior his deeds in the gentleness of wisdom. But if you have bitter jealousy and selfish ambition in your heart, do not be arrogant and so lie against the truth. This wisdom is not that which comes down from above, but is earthly, natural, demonic. For where jealousy and selfish ambition exist, there is disorder and every evil thing. But the wisdom from above is first pure, then peaceable, gentle, reasonable, full of mercy and good fruits, unwavering, without hypocrisy.

Wow! What a great way to evaluate our parenting! Is our wisdom gentle? Going back to our first chapter, gentleness is such a crucial element in raising God's girls. When we bring wisdom to our daughters, is in a spirit of gentleness?

In this passage we also see a startling contrast. We can share wisdom with our daughters, but it can be earthly, natural, or demonic. What? Is our advice earthly, based on the latest teaching in this month's parenting magazine? *The article said I need to let my 5-year-old discover her own god instead of teaching her about the God in Scripture.* Is our advice natural, based on our own preferences? *I was the oldest child so I know what it feels like to have to do the most work, so I'm not going to make my daughter do chores around the house.* Or is our advice demonic, based on the falsehoods of the Father of Lies (John 8:44). *You're a spoiled brat. Why do I bother; you're never going to change?*

Instead, is our wisdom pure? This includes our advice, our comments, our encouragement, and our correction. Do we truly want to help our daughters be all they can be in the Lord? Is it peaceable and gentle, not harming our relationship but actually building our relationship stronger as our daughter feels that we are "for her?"

Is our counsel reasonable? Is our counsel driven by the clear teaching of Scripture or driven by our own raging mood swings? Is our advice full of mercy? Do we openly share ways we have struggled in similar circumstances and encourage growth with empathy? Are we bearing good fruit? Are our daughters learning and growing from our input?

Are we unwavering in our convictions? Do we stand on Scripture when it's easy and when it's hard? When we tell our daughters we parent according to Scripture, do we reference this only when we discipline them, or do we reference this also when we choose to hang out with them and remind them that they are gifts from the Lord and that He wants us to enjoy them and bless them?

And finally, are we hypocrites? What a stumbling block this can be. Are we the same in the home and outside the home? Do we live for the Lord as we train our daughters to do the same? Do they see us rolling our eyes at our husbands and being rude and mocking, while expecting them to be respectful to us?

What great questions to ask ourselves and evaluate our hearts. If our actions are not lining up with these Scriptures, according to James the cause can be selfish ambition or jealousy of others or even jealousy of our daughters. We can ask God to examine our hearts, and get thoughts from those that know us well.

Fellow mom, if the Holy Spirit has brought any conviction here, James 3:14 exhorts us to not be arrogant and lie against the truth. Cling to I John 1:9, "If we confess our sins, he is faithful and righteous to forgive us our sins and to cleanse us from all unrighteousness." Receive the Lord's forgiveness and cleansing, confess where needed to your husband and daughters, and now walk in truth. You will benefit and so will your daughters as they watch you respond to biblical conviction, fight your sin, and embrace the truths of Scripture. They will learn from your example of biblical womanhood, and they will benefit from the fruit of your changed life.

Hormones

Now for the final pitfall...Hormones. The mood swings, the apathy, the sharp tongue, the rolling eyes...oh, and that's just us moms! Add to that our daughters' struggles and we have a boiling cauldron about to erupt. We'll talk a little more about hormones in Chapter 5, but they certainly need to be mentioned here.

We have four daughters and my own hormones are still active and changing daily. Five women with fluctuating hormones! It's a miracle my husband and sons survive! Here's a few things I've learned along the way:

- Keep track of your daughter's periods. I have a calendar where I track their cycles and mine. This has been so helpful.

Hormones are real and they affect each daughter differently. Stephanie had been talking with her dad for over an hour and I could hear her crying on and off. The problem? Her younger brother had used the toaster oven when it was her turn. I walked over to the calendar, checked if it was almost time for her period, nodded to my husband, and walked out of the room.

See, my husband has also been informed. He grew up with no sisters, so he learned with me and my daughters. We have both learned to be gracious to our daughters during these cyclical struggles. To evaluate the situation based on this knowledge and not overreact or make any rash judgments based on their words at this time.

- My daughters and I have learned to give head and neck massages during this time—and to give chocolate as needed.

- I have learned that my words will have a more bitter tone when I am struggling with PMS, so during these seasons I try not to bring up any new topics of correction and keep my words to a minimum. "When there are many words, transgression is unavoidable, but he who restrains his lips is wise" (Prov. 10:19).

- And I have learned that it serves everyone if we know when someone is not feeling well. I let my daughters know: *I have quite a headache today. So if I seem less than enthusiastic, please don't take it personally.* If we don't let others know the source of our attitude, then they are likely to think it has something to do with them, and they will carry unnecessary guilt.

All this said, we as women, of any age, do not have permission to sin just because our hormones are raging. I've checked, but Galatians 5 does not say, "these are the fruits of the Spirit if you are *not* having your period." There's no escape clause, and let's not teach our daughters there is. Let's teach them to recognize the increased temptation during this time and to spend more time praying, stretching, taking hot showers, drinking herbal teas to ease the pain, and asking each other for prayer. *Hormones may rage in our home, but they don't have to rule!*

A Quilt of Encouragement

We must be so careful here, especially with our daughter's hearts when it comes to their appearance. The world tries to tell our daughters that they need to look a certain way. Our girls are daily bombarded by billboards, magazines, television commercials, and Internet ads telling them how they need to change their bodies to make them beautiful. Even in school or among friends, they are often criticized or mocked. It is truly a battleground.

Our homes need to be places of refuge and refreshment from this constant attack. When our daughters come in from the cold world that judges them based on their appearance, we need to offer them a quilt of encouragement. A quilt pieced together with truths from Scripture and sincere compliments. We need to cover our daughters in the truth that they are beautiful because they are made in the image of God. We need to highlight how God intentionally created each girl to look different and cultivate in them the confidence to see beauty in themselves and to see beauty in their friends. We can create a culture at home filled with compliments: *Wow, your hair looks great. That color is wonderful on you. God gave you such a beautiful smile.* Encouraging our daughters in this area will not only help their own personal confidence but also help them to do the same for their friends and create a circle of girls that truly care for each other and sincerely compliment and build each other up. It's a win-win!

Francine: Mom, did you see this pimple on my chin? It looks terrible.

Mom: Yeah, I saw it. Cover it up with some make-up and I'll call the dermatologist today. We need to get rid of that thing!

Message to daughter: Mom wants to help me look good.

Francine: Mom, did you see this pimple on my chin? It looks terrible.

Mom: Let me see. Yeah, I see one growing there. I will get you some medication tonight, and if that doesn't help, I'll take you to the dermatologist if you want. But I tell you what. With beautiful eyes like yours, nobody's going to pay attention to a little bump on your face.

Message: Mom wants to help me, and she thinks I'm beautiful

Our relationships with our daughters are built on hundreds of conversations like these. And a culmination of many, many small messages leaves a big message in our daughters' hearts. Our daughters will be blessed as we intentionally look for ways to encourage them daily.

Moms, we must not reflect the world's teachings in this area. A world that has a narrow, specific definition of physical beauty and believes that any price is worth paying to achieve this goal. We must value our daughters' hearts for this is what God looks at (1 Samuel 16:7), while we regularly remind our daughters that they are fearfully and wonderfully made, doing all we can to help their souls know this well. Let us not be another voice that criticizes them, placing unnecessary standards on them based on our personal preferences. Our daughters get enough of this from others. Let's do all we can to build them up.

Are We Filling Our Daughters With Sinful Pride or Godly Confidence?

Wait a minute! We're Christians. What's all this talk about building confidence in our daughters? James 4:6 tells us that, "God is opposed to the proud, but gives grace to the humble." I don't want to teach my daughter to be proud; that's just setting her up for opposition from the Lord.

Great question! What is the difference between being proud and being confident? *Pride is based on comparison to others; confidence is based on the truth of God's Word.*

In Galatians 6:3-4, we see that we are not to compare ourselves to others. "For if anyone thinks he is something when he is nothing, he deceives himself. But each one must examine his own work, and then he will have reason for boasting in regard to himself alone, and not in regard to another." Pride is reflected in sinful comparison. *I can't believe she wore that; I wouldn't be caught dead in an outfit like that....She is so wrapped up in herself; she's never once comes with me to the nursing home on Saturday mornings....You think we should do another carwash? I have some much more creative ideas to raise money for our youth group.*

Even our counsel to our daughters can stir up prideful comparisons.

Ginger: I didn't get chosen to sing in the Christmas Cantata!
After all that practice! They loved Rosalie's song, though,
and she gets the main part! That's just not fair.

Mom: I'm sorry, Honey. But you know Rosalie is really not that pretty, so it's good she'll get this little bit of attention. I tell you what. Let's go shopping and we'll get you a beautiful new dress to wear to the Cantata. You may not be singing, but you'll be prettier than all the girls there!

Message: I'm prettier than all the other girls,
and that's what's most important.

Ginger: I didn't get chosen to sing in the Christmas Cantata!
After all that practice! They loved Rosalie's song, though,
and she gets the main part! That's just not fair.

Mom: Honey, I'm sorry you didn't make it. I know you worked really hard
on that song. Rosalie does have a beautiful voice, and I look forward to
hearing her sing. Maybe there's another way you can serve at the Cantata.
What about being a greeter? God has given you that amazing smile that
lights up a room; you'd be great at welcoming people to the service.

Message: I have a variety of giftings from God that I can use for Him.

We need to remember that we are not to draw our confidence from putting others down and pumping ourselves up. We are to draw our confidence from being God's Girl - fearfully and wonderfully made.

Encouragement and Enjoyment Walk Hand in Hand

As we fight these common pitfalls…not embracing our biblical role, carrying and giving worldly guilt, treating preferences as sin, fear, jealousy, and unaddressed hormones…and as we grow in encouraging our daughter, we will discover an amazing fruit: we enjoy our daughters more and they enjoy us more.

Who doesn't like hanging out with someone who thinks you're wonderful?

Let's let our daughters know they are amazing. Let's encourage them, and honor them to their faces and behind their backs. Let's point out attributes we admire and quickly admit areas where we can grow from their examples. Let's seek their help in their areas of expertise and seek their prayers and counsel when we struggle.

Let's welcome their interruptions. *Mommy, can you get this shoe off my doll? Mommy, can you help me find the red crayon I used yesterday? Mommy, come look at the sunset! Mom, can you help me with school? Mom, guess who I saw at the mall today?*

Though my own mom worked hard to support us and run our household, she always made time to listen to me and take an interest in my life. This began when I was young, and continued as I grew up, so that I generally didn't keep secrets from her; no matter how bad my life was, she pretty much knew what I was doing. My mom gave me a precious gift: her time and attention.

When our daughters enter a room, may we smile and make eye contact. May they walk in security among family friends knowing that we are not slandering them. May we delight in their talents and giftings and delight in the ways they are different than us.

And may we laugh together! A joyful heart is good medicine (Proverbs 17:22). Let's tell funny stories from our childhood. Let's laugh at ourselves regularly, not hiding our mistakes, but quickly admitting them with a light heart and a big smile. *So, Christine, when I asked you to make spaghetti tonight, it would have been helpful if I had checked to see if we had any sauce. I guess it's bagels for dinner tonight thanks to my "superior planning skills."* We don't need to be afraid to admit our mistakes or sins. Our daughters see them anyway. We're not telling them something they don't already know.

Play games together, watch movies together, make crafts together, walk together, play dolls together, study the Bible together. Share jokes, share stories, share fears, share triumphs. Share life. Because encouraging and enjoying as described in Deuteronomy requires a shared life....walking along the way together. The more we encourage; the more we enjoy.

Life is a seamless conversation and relationship that begins the minute you conceive (or welcome an adopted daughter into your life) and continues through changes and challenges, growing each season and building on the foundation of the prior season. One day you're playing house with your daughter, the next day you're at the store helping her pick out decorations for her new home. It really goes that fast! Oh, Mom, let's enjoy these years and diligently fight all that comes against our precious relationships with our daughters.

You Are Mom!

Mom, you have a high calling. A difficult calling. An important calling. You need to walk in the confidence that it is the Lord that has called you to be a mother, and He will give you "everything pertaining to life and godliness through the true knowledge of Him" (2 Peter 1:3).

Embrace your calling, Mom. At the workplace, though you may do a wonderful job, you can be replaced. On that church committee, your administration is valuable, but you can be replaced. On that internet group, your comments are insightful, but you can be replaced.

Your daughter will have many friends throughout her life; but she will only have one Mom. You are irreplaceable! You are Mom, the one and only. Be the Mom, and enjoy your gift from God!

Prayer

Lord, help me to nurture and comfort my daughter. May I lead by example and instruct her and never throw a blanket of worldly guilt upon her. Let fear not hold me back from parenting her according to Your Word. Let me both encourage her and enjoy my time with her as I walk in the role that You have given me.

The Daughters Speak

Katie Says...

I wanted to write for this chapter when I first read the title, "Like Mother, Like Daughter." In many ways I am like my mom, and in most of the areas where I'm not, I want to become like her. When asked what I want to be when I get older, I always reply, "I want to be a homeschooling mom like my mom!" Believe me, if I could be even half as great a wife and mom as she is, I would be doing pretty fantastic. My mom is just that awesome (and no she did not put me up to this)!

The other reason I wanted to write on this chapter was because there have been many instances where my parents could've thrown worldly guilt on me but have chosen not to. For example, when I was about ten or eleven years old I loved to skateboard. I would practice a lot and my apparel would have a modest, but skateboard-ish look to it. I even chose a cool nickname for myself, K-dawg! My parents didn't mind that my interests were different than my older sisters. They encouraged me in the little tricks that I could do. They bought me a skateboard ramp and even got me a hat that said "K-dawg."

One day I asked my mom if I could get a second ear piercing to match the earrings already in my ear. She didn't respond by telling me that it was a crazy idea. Instead, she told me that if I would like a second piercing I would need to start dressing more feminine, like sometimes wearing dresses to church. She didn't want there to be a rough look about me; that did not reflect my personality and would not be a great representation of the joy of Christ in my life. I immediately started wearing dresses to church (and started to like it), and in a couple of years she and Dad surprised me with a gift to go and get my second piercing.

Another example is that right now I love to dress anywhere from rocker cute to cowgirl! You can find me with a sparkly shirt and sneakers or a plaid shirt with brown boots. My parents never make me feel guilty for dressing like a cowgirl when all my peers are dressed sporty. Modesty is a huge deal, though. I am confident that if my parents tell me that I am not allowed to wear a certain outfit, it is not because it is their preference—it is either immodest or not suited for the occasion.

They are very strict with matters of the heart. There are many parties my friends can go to, or movies they watch, that I can't because my parents want to guard my heart. They go out of their way to protect my heart, for from it flows the springs of life (Prov. 4:23). They encourage me that my heart is worth protecting. They don't correct style, the color of nail polish, and other expressions of personality (unless, of course, our personality is reflecting a sin pattern!). But they do quickly and lovingly correct sin. They always check for the motive behind why we are acting or dressing a certain way. They encourage us when we make the right choice. My mom has always made it clear that when I dye my hair or put on make-up or get another piercing, it is never to hide who I am but to accent and enhance the beauty God has already given me.

Remember the example about the girl who came to her mom worried about a pimple on her face? Yeah, that would be me. Remember the second example of the mom's response? Yes, that would be my mom's words to me. On many occasions I have come to my mom worried about acne on my face. She would always reply, "Oh, I am sorry. I bet it hurts. I can put some medicine on it tonight. But you know what, God has given you such beautiful eyes no one will pay attention to that little pimple on your face." I would always come away from a conversation like that feeling very loved, confident, beautiful, and thankful. I knew that even though I might have a break-out on my face, I was made in God's image, my mom thought I was beautiful, and my daddy always hugged me and complimented me, no matter how I looked. It didn't really matter what anyone else thought! I was God's girl!

My parents have never made me feel guilty for wanting to try new things. They never made me feel guilty for spilling pineapple juice on the floor or breaking the chair in the living room or accidently breaking the window in the schoolroom...oh, the list goes on and on! Sin, on the other hand, is sin. I need to feel the godly sorrow that leads to repentance when I have disobeyed. I am called to have a pure heart, dress modestly, and be a witness to the world of Christ's love in my life. When I confess my sin to my parents, I know they will forgive me. When I have a new outfit or new idea for my hair, I know they will never dismiss it based on their own preferences but based on God's Word that I am to be light unto the world and shine like a star (Matt. 5:16 and Phil. 2:14-15).

All this to say, I love my parents so much! I am so grateful for the way they have guarded my heart and stood firm on the truth of God's Word about issues of the heart. I am also thankful for the way they have never made me feel guilty for my God-given personality. I can walk with confidence in my cowgirl boots with my brown/blonde hair, even if I have a pimple on my face, because I know I am God's girl and my parents love me and support me.

3

That's My Princess

The Importance of a Father's Love

As I walk in the door, I am greeted by a little girl in a rumpled pink dance costume.

"Sit down, Daddy," she says as she pulls me to the couch. "I have a dance to show you."

The worship song begins to play, and my daughter starts to twirl and leap, eagerly glancing over at me throughout her performance. At the end, she stops, breathless and waiting. Waiting for my response. Waiting for me to clap. Waiting to hear it was beautiful. Waiting to hear that she is beautiful.

I smile and wipe the tears from my eyes. Oh, yes, the dance was beautiful. And yes, my daughter is beautiful. I lavish words of praise on her. I want her to know I cherish these moments, and I cherish her.

Each daughter starts out with a deep longing to know her daddy. She wants to be his Princess. She wants him to think that she is beautiful and worth fighting for. She wants to know that his love for her is unconditional, that he will encourage her when she is downcast, and challenge and guide her when she strays. In short, she wants him to reflect the heart of God.

In *Captivating*, John and Stasi Eldredge write,

Every little girl was made to live in a world with a father who loves her unconditionally. She first learns who God is, what He is like, and how He feels about her from her earthly dad. God is 'Our Father, who art in heaven.' He means initially to reveal Himself to His daughters and His sons through the love of our dads. We were meant to know a father's love, be kept safe in it, be protected by it, and blossom there.[1]

What Comes between a Father and Daughter?

Sadly, however, there are many forces that oppose a girl's God-given desire to be close to her father. For example, look at what today's media teaches through movie themes. Daughter wants to do something extreme. Dad says no. Daughter disobeys and does it anyway. Dad is upset. Daughter succeeds. Dad says he was wrong. The message: Dad's an idiot.

Our sin nature is also against us. We can tend to tilt between two extremes. On the one end, we want to be involved and we end up trying to direct every detail of our daughters' lives. As a result, they become exasperated. Or, at the other end of the spectrum, we choose to check out and become passive. This leaves our daughters unprotected and exposed.

Also, there is an enemy named Satan that opposes us. According to John 10:10, his work is to steal, kill, and destroy. He wants to steal away your daughter's heart, kill her desire to be close to you, and destroy her relationship with God. First Peter 5:8 says this enemy is like a roaring lion seeking someone to devour.

God is For Us

Yet despite all this opposition, we can be confident that God is for us and He has given us all we need to be successful in raising our daughters. This truth is wonderfully captured in Romans 8:31b-32, which says, "…If God is for us, who can be against us? He who did not spare his own Son, but gave him up for us all—how will he not also, along with him, graciously give us all things?" (NIV).

Let's look at the first part of this passage. "If God is for us, who can be against us?" This is a rhetorical question; the obvious answer is that no one can be against us and prevail when God is on our side. It doesn't matter how difficult the situation seems or how impossible you think it is to resolve, God is greater.

In addition, the second part of the passage says that He will "graciously give us all things." A parallel passage in 2 Peter 1:3 says, "His divine power has granted to us everything pertaining to life and godliness, through the true knowledge of Him who called us by His own glory and excellence." The bottom line is this: God has given us everything we need to raise our daughters for His glory! No matter what our childhood was like, or how limited our education was, or how inadequate we feel, God has given us everything we need.

Look at this description from Scripture on how a father should inspire his children: "just as you know how we were exhorting and encouraging and imploring each one of you *as a father would his own children*, so that you would walk in a manner worthy of the God who calls you into His own kingdom and glory" (1 Thess. 2:11-12, emphasis added).

It is God's desire that our hearts be with our daughters. "Behold, I am going to send you Elijah the prophet before the coming of the great and terrible day of the LORD. He will restore the hearts of the fathers to their children and the hearts of the children to their fathers, so that I will not come and smite the land with a curse" (Mal. 4:5-6). Notice which comes first: restore the hearts of the fathers to the children, then the children's hearts follow.

We can do this! We can communicate to our daughter that she is a Princess, that she is beautiful, and that our love for her is unconditional. We can uphold her and pray that she will "be strong in the Lord and in the strength of His might" (Eph. 6:10). We can bring encouragement to her when she is downcast, and correction and guidance to her when she sins. And the reason we can do all these things has absolutely nothing to do with any natural ability we possess, but it is entirely because God has given us all we need. So, with confident expectation, we can seek Him for wisdom and strength in raising His girls.

How Can I Show Love to My Daughter?

Have you ever heard of the book *Everything Men Know About Women*? It's 120 pages long...and all the pages are blank![2]

Truly, women are a mystery to most men. For some of us, the word *emotions* elicits such great fear that it either sends us running for cover or causes us to freeze like a deer caught in the headlights. We tend to be light on the emotional side and heavy on the rational side. This does not lend itself to being great listeners when our daughters are struggling with emotions that don't need practical answers.

Yet caring for our daughters' hearts is probably the most important area for us to focus on if we really want to deepen our relationships with them and help them grow in the Lord. Proverbs 20:5 says, "The purpose in a man's heart is like deep water, but a man of understanding will draw it out" (ESV). Proverbs 4:23 says, "Watch over your heart with all diligence, For from it flow the springs of life." *God places a priority on the heart; so should we.*

Caring for our daughters' hearts is a powerful expression of love. Below are seven ways we can do this.

1. Respect the Differences between Girls and Boys

If we want to care for our daughters' hearts, a great place to begin is in understanding the differences between boys and girls. Our first four children were girls, so I had become familiar with the sweet feminine side of little girls. Then along came the boys—three of them. And it did not take long to realize that there were some big differences.

The contrast between our sons and daughters can be easily seen any time we are getting ready to go somewhere as a family. Our daughters will spend much time trying on outfits, styling their hair, making sure everything looks right. They come and ask for input on what they are wearing. For my boys, I feel like getting them to comb their hair is the same as pulling teeth. They can be ready to go in virtually no time with mismatched clothes and dirty faces and not care at all how they look.

When they were younger, our girls loved to play dress up, have tea parties, and create dance recitals. For many years, until we had our first boy, we used to have annual "Sisters' Day" celebrations where our daughters would invite their friends over and have a party. At these events, you would often see me dressed up as a goofy waiter that took everything literally (like a male version of Amelia Bedelia). With a hand-drawn mustache and a pillow under my shirt to expand my waist size, I was responsible for food and drinks at the party. If they asked for tea, I wrote a letter "T" and gave it to them. If they asked for a hot dog, I would toss a stuffed dog in the microwave and then serve it on a plate. My daughters and their friends totally loved it! We had a great time.

However, if I ever donned a similar costume around my boys, they would probably say, "Look, Dad stuffed a pillow under his shirt and painted a mustache on his face so he could be a funny-looking punching bag. Let's pounce on him!" You see, boys want to conquer, they want to win battles. No matter what the topic or who the opponent, my nine-year-old son always thinks he is the smartest, strongest, and fastest (guess our teaching on humility hasn't kicked in yet). I'm just as guilty. It's hard to walk by my boys and not intentionally bump into them and knock them into the couch and start a wrestling match as my wife cringes in the background.

Why does it matter if I understand the difference between boys and girls? Because I'm a boy! The differences I can easily see between the genders in my children arc also alive between me and my daughters. After all, my heart is not that much different than it was when I was a ten-year-old boy, as my wife will attest. Being aware of these differences keeps me from evaluating situations based totally on what I think, instead of respecting the feminine heart.

Skyler: Daddy, I can't get my pigtails even.
This one is always higher than the other.

Daddy (glancing up from his paper): What difference does it make?

You're just going to be playing in the backyard anyway.

Message: Daddy doesn't care about me.

Skyler: Daddy, I can't get my pigtails even.
This one is always higher than the other.

Daddy (looking up and setting his paper on the couch):
Well, let me see how I can help. I've got this ponytail thing down
pretty good. Let's see if I can learn to do pigtails too.

Message: Daddy cares about me.

❖ ❖ ❖

For those of you dads who wanted a son but got a daughter, please don't tell your daughter that you wish she was a boy. You may not think it is a big deal, but it is very hurtful to a young girl's heart. Instead, let her know how blessed you are to have her. Pour out love and kindness to her. She is truly a gift from God. If you choose to complain about having a daughter or grumble in your heart that she is not a boy, what you are really saying is this: *God, You made a mistake.* Recognize that at the root of your perspective is pride; you are ultimately saying that you know better than God. Repent and embrace your daughter as a beautiful gift from God.

2. Look at Your Daughter through God's Eyes

Pause for a moment and think about the lens that you use to view your daughter. Philippians 4:8 says, "Finally, brothers, whatever is true, whatever is honorable, whatever is just, whatever is pure, whatever is lovely, whatever is commendable, if there is any excellence, if there is anything worthy of praise, think about these things" (ESV). This is God's lens; is it yours?

For example, if you dwell on a co-worker's negative qualities, you may conclude that he is a critical killjoy. Whatever he says will come through this lens, and you will probably try to avoid him. On the other hand, if you look at this same person through a biblical lens, you will see him as someone who has not experienced the love of God and His forgiveness. Compassion can then well up in your heart when you see him. This can motivate you to pray and demonstrate tangible expressions of love to penetrate the hardness that has encased him. Same person, same issues— different lens, different response.

Likewise, the way we view our daughters will profoundly influence the way we relate to them. Suppose your daughter is going through a period where she is being inconsiderate and self-focused. If you view her as a rude, selfish whiner that cares only about herself, then that is how you will treat her. It may also lead to roots of bitterness growing in your heart. However, if you see her as a princess in need of rescue from her spiritual blindness and the grip of the enemy, then you can rise up and engage in spiritual warfare on her behalf.

Carrie: Dad! You left the car on empty again! Can't you just fill it up on your way home? Now, I'll probably be late to work!

Dad: What is your problem? If you don't like the way I manage my car, then here's a radical idea: buy your own!

Message: I can't talk to my dad about anything!

Carrie: Dad! You left the car on empty again! Can't you just fill it up on your way home? Now, I'll probably be late to work!

Dad: Oh, man. I really meant to check it on the way home. I'd much rather you have a full tank before you head out to work at night.

Carrie: Well, can you not let it happen again?

Dad: Sure, I'll try to remember. But you know what, Carrie?
Next time you don't have to come at me in such an attack mode.
You could just say: "Dad, I'm really glad you let me use your car.
If you could fill it up on the way home, though, I'd feel a lot safer
driving to work." I try not to speak harshly to you and you
don't need to speak harshly to me either. Okay, Honey?

Message: My dad is for me. He wants me safe,
and he wants me to learn to communicate well.

What do you see in your daughter that is true, honorable, just, pure, lovely, commendable, excellent, or praiseworthy? Think on these things! Then we will be positioned to grow in love and compassion for our daughters rather than in bitterness and disdain. Our daughters are God's girls and we need to choose to see them through His eyes.

3. Enter Her World

Armed with an understanding and appreciation of the unique qualities of girls and having the right picture of our daughters in our minds, we are better prepared to enter her world—to discover what she enjoys doing and do it with her. This is a great way to communicate our love for our daughters in a tangible way. Now, this may not come easy. I mean how many dads really enjoy playing Barbies? *We participate not because we love the activity, but because we love our daughters.*

We first need to discover what our daughters like, which is often not very hard. Simply listen to what she regularly asks you to do with her. As she gets older and her interests change, you may need to ask some questions to discover what she likes most.

*Dad: Hey, Stacy, I just got back from deer hunting
and got me a big buck. Want to help me skin and gut it?*

Stacy: Yuck, Dad. That's disgusting!

*Dad: Look, your mom's all over me for not spending
enough time with you. Don't say I didn't try.*

Message: Dad does not understand me at all.

*Dad: Hey, Stacy, I just got back from deer hunting
and got me a big buck. Want to help me skin and gut it?*

Stacy: Yuck, Dad. That's disgusting!

*Dad: Yeah, I wasn't sure if you'd want to help me. How about this?
At dinner last night I heard you mention a new smoothie place
that opened. How about when I finish up with the deer,
you and I go check it out? Drinks on me!*

Message: My dad wants to understand me.

When my daughters were younger, playing make-believe with dolls was the norm. As they got a little older, I would join in on fun pranks they played on their younger siblings. Now that my daughters are teenage and above, you might find me traveling to Alaska with one of my daughters or taking another shopping at the mall. Regardless of the activity, the message to our daughters is still the same when we participate: you are special and I love spending time with you.

My friend, Ben, was taking out the trash with his three-year-old daughter when she looked at the moon and said, "Daddy, I want one. Will you get one for me?" He could have just brushed her question aside with, "No, that's not possible, Honey." But instead when they went inside, he took advantage of this opportunity to show her several YouTube videos about the moon. She loved it, and it sent a clear message to her that what was important to her, was important to Daddy.

Playing with our daughters is not just an opportunity to make them feel loved; it's also a great opportunity to impart biblical truths. Sean, pastor and father of three, says he views playing with his five-year-old daughter as a way to demonstrate biblical manhood—so she won't be duped by a counterfeit when she gets older! When she declared, "Daddy, knights always beat up the bad guys so the princesses can sit around and do nothing," he responded by explaining that the knight's role is to protect the princess, which does not always involve beating someone up. And the knight does not protect the princess so she can just sit around and do nothing; the knight protects her so that the princess is free to do all that God has called her to do without fear. Whether playing knight, king, or superhero, Sean is an archetype of God the Father.

Our oldest daughter, Brittany, took ballet lessons from age six to thirteen. She loved to dance and she loved to go to dance performances. She especially loved to watch the older girls from her studio that were part of the "company" dance team. One time, I surprised her with a date night to go to their performance at a local church. She absolutely loved it and still remembers it to this day as being a very special time with Dad. What's funny is I never would have thought this would have been so meaningful to her. But I sure am glad that we went.

Another way to enter your daughter's world is to become friends with her friends. Think about the last time your daughter had a friend over. What was your level of interaction? Was it the perfunctory, "Hi, how are you?" or did you take time to get to know him or her? Take an interest in their lives and ask follow-up questions next time. Invite the friends to stay for dinner and share funny stories. Draw the friends into your family life and look for opportunities to encourage your daughter's friends in the Lord. It blesses your daughter and makes her more likely to bring friends to your home.

Our role is crucial. We are modeling the fatherly heart of God. We want our daughters to know that just like we can go to God at any time and He hears us, so our daughters can come to us at any time and we will listen to them. If we find ourselves regularly saying no to our daughters' requests to "enter their world," we need to go to God in prayer and ask Him to help make this a priority. The more we enter their world and share with them what they enjoy, the better we can care for their hearts.

Time spent joining a tea party with dolls may one day become a date night at her favorite restaurant. Playing "Go Fish" with your five-year-old can transform into being card partners when she's fifteen. Watching children's videos with her as a toddler can grow into her inviting you to join her and her friend as they head to the movies. All these seemingly insignificant activities translate to one loud and clear message to your daughter: You are special, and I love spending time with you. This may then return to you: Dad, you are special, and I love spending time with you.

4. Bring Her Into Your World

What's your spiritual passion, Dad? Do you have a desire to feed the poor, raise money for missions work, or start a prayer ministry? Maybe your spiritual gifting is administrative, and you want to help your church get better organized. How can you bring your daughter along with you as you seek to fulfill God's call on your life? This will not only increase your effectiveness; it will also help her to be better prepared as a helpmate for a husband (Gen. 2:18). By helping you pursue the spiritual goals God has given you, she is learning how to be a better helper, and in the process your relationship with her is growing stronger as you co-labor together.

My primary spiritual passion is local evangelism. I love talking with strangers about their spiritual beliefs, answering questions about Christianity, and explaining the gospel. From the time my daughters were babies, I involved them in this passion. They have come with me to hand out flyers in neighborhoods inviting folks to church events. They have joined me in doing door-to-door evangelism and street witnessing. They have participated in classes that I have taught on evangelism. As a result, my daughters are comfortable starting conversations with strangers and explaining what they believe.

Here's an interesting note: My wife was once talking to a mom who grew up with a dad that also evangelized regularly and took his children with him. "Wow, that's great," my wife responded enthusiastically.

The woman shook her head. "No, not really. I pretty much dreaded it." My wife went home saddened as she thought about this woman's comment. She prayed about it, sought out the woman the next week, and asked why her perspective was so negative.

"Well," the woman said. "I've seen your husband with your children and it's obvious that they have a great relationship. I think that's what was missing—relationship. It was just an activity that my dad wanted to do, and we didn't really have a close relationship in any other ways."

She added another insight. "I think another issue was my friends. None of them went out evangelizing, and I was pretty dependent on their opinions at that age."

Peer pressure can work for you or against you. Help your daughter choose friends that enhance her relationship with the Lord and her relationship with you. One who scoffs at your involvement in your daughter's life should not be in your home and should not be considered a friend. Instead, invite your daughter's true friends into all aspects of your family life, and include them in outreaches and other ministries on your heart.

When the leaders of our church asked me to develop and lead an evangelistic outreach that involved a free dinner, apologetic/evangelistic message, and small group discussion over multiple weeks, I asked my daughter, Brittany, to help. She was about eighteen at the time and working at our church office. She handled the entire administrative part of this program and did an outstanding job. It was a great time of co-laboring together, but even more, the event was a huge success because of her involvement.

Book studies are a great way to involve your daughter in your spiritual passion. For high school, we assigned the book, *Will Our Generation Speak? A Call to be Bold with the Gospel* by Grace Malley.[3] Then we invited other people to also read the book and join us for a weekly dinner and discussion. Another dad, several of our children, as well as some of their friends, participated in the eight-week study. We had a great time together.

God has also put on my heart a desire to rescue babies, so we take our daughters to abortion centers and reach out to the women there. We brought our daughters even when they were young. This really had a positive impact on them and now all four of them have strong pro-life perspectives. In fact, my oldest daughter and her husband have been caring for a foster baby, which is a wonderful expression of their pro-life convictions.

My friend, Brian, has a passion for teaching and he started a homeschool co-op. Rather than hiring all outside teachers, his children teach classes. As a result, his children have grown in their teaching skills and have grown closer to Dad as they work together to make the school successful.

Maybe you're not sure where to start involving your daughter in your spiritual passion. That's okay, start with something simple. Practicing hospitality has been an outstanding way to co-labor with my daughters. As we have opened our home to people both inside and outside of the church, our girls have had many opportunities to grow. When they were young, they learned how to share their toys with other children that were visiting. As they got older, they learned how to make conversation with guests and help with food prep, getting drinks, or giving a tour of the house. What I find most rewarding, though, is when we spend time praying and our daughters share scriptures and words of encouragement with our guests.

Another great way to involve our daughters in our lives is through our hobbies. What do you enjoy doing? Do you like to paint, work with wood, fish, or run? Think about how you can get your daughter involved.

I like to surf. I had not really surfed much after college, but one summer I borrowed a friend's surfboard and took it to the beach. My daughters wanted to try and two of them really enjoyed it, so I began teaching them how to surf. In fact, Stephanie asked for a surfboard for her birthday. Sometimes your hobby becomes your daughter's hobby, which makes sharing life even better.

Beyond spiritual passions and hobbies, we can also look for simple ways to bring our daughters into our world. For example, my mom had given me a remote control helicopter. One night I invited Stephanie to join me in learning to fly the helicopter in the living room. Our first competition was to see who could keep it in the air the longest. She went for over two minutes; I crashed before I reached forty seconds. We had a great time together. Simple moments can make super memories.

5. Let Your Helpmate Help

Dad, does all this seem overwhelming to you? Many of us were never taught how to care for a girl's heart. If you, like me, had no sisters growing up, you may feel like you are especially clueless.

Well, take heart; if you have a wife, then you have a clue! God has given us helpmates. Your wife can help you understand the heart of a girl because she is a girl. She can relate to your daughter's emotions and give valuable insight.

This has happened on numerous occasions in our household, with my wife prepping me in advance of a conversation with one of my daughters. "Honey, Stephanie wants to talk to you about an incident that happened today with her brother. Keep in mind that it is 'that time of the month' and she's a little weepy." Without Mary Lou's upfront comments, my conversation with Stephanie may have been very short and ended with me insensitively declaring, "Wow, that's a pretty insignificant issue. Why in the world would you let that bother you?"

But now, armed with feminine insight into the situation, I approach it differently. The conversation lasts longer because I give Stephanie time to share what is on her heart. I listen to what she is saying and ask sensitive questions. By the time the conversation is done, the situation is usually resolved and my daughter feels better. The end result has absolutely nothing to do with my brilliant counseling skills, but everything to do with my wife prepping me.

Not only can your wife help you understand your daughter, but your daughter can help you understand your wife! Here are some typical examples in our home:

- My wife is wearing a new shirt and Katie comes up to me and says, "Hey Dad, did you notice Mom has a new shirt on?"

- It's Saturday and getting near lunchtime, and my wife makes a comment about there not being much food in the house. *Well there's always something that can be pulled together for lunch,* I think. However, one of my daughters comes to me and whispers, "I think Mom is asking you to pick up some Chick-Fil-A for lunch."

Let's be thankful for the women in our home and learn from *all* of them.

6. Speak Tenderly

It's instructive that there are only two explicit directives in the New Testament to fathers on how they should treat their children. In Colossians 3:21, we are told, "Fathers, do not exasperate your children, so that they will not lose heart." Ephesians 6:4 says, "Fathers, do not provoke your children to anger, but bring them up in the discipline and instruction of the Lord." One of the primary ways that we exasperate and provoke our children is by expressing anger towards them.

Sometimes we can be uncertain how to handle a difficult situation with our daughters. We might not be sure what to say to resolve the issue, but one thing we can know for certain: speaking harshly is never the right answer. Colossians 3:19 says, "Husbands, love your wives, and do not be harsh with them" (ESV). While this passage is focused on the marriage relationship, it is instructive that women are especially hurt by harsh words.

It's amazing how responsive our daughters can be when we speak tenderly. Stephanie asked me last night to wake her up at 6:15 a.m. to get ready for work. So I set an alarm on my phone for her with a message that read, "Wake up, sweet Stephanie" and set it next to her bed. I was out jogging when the alarm went off. Later in the morning before I went to work, she had a big smile on her face and thanked me for the message. Four simple words…not even spoken…touched her heart. Really, it was the one word *sweet* that did it. This took me maybe one minute max to accomplish.

7. Listen to Your Daughter's Input

How do you respond to observations from your daughter? Can she bring you her thoughts about areas you may need to change without you getting upset? Does she know that you will take her comments seriously and go to the Lord in prayer? Or do you try to defend yourself and make excuses? The way we respond to correction reveals our maturity (or lack thereof).

Julie: Dad, you don't care about what is important to me.

Dad: What do you mean I don't care about what is important to you?

Julie: You interrupt me when I am sharing and change the topic to what you want to discuss. Like last night when I tried to talk with you about getting my driver's license.

Dad: If you weren't so busy all the time, I wouldn't need to do this. But because you seldom seem to have time to talk, I need to make the most of the opportunities.

Message: Dad does not care about what is important to me.

Julie: Dad, you don't care about what is important to me.

Dad: What makes you feel that way, Honey?

*Julie: You interrupt me when I am sharing and change the topic
to what you want to discuss. Like last night when I tried to
talk with you about getting my driver's license.*

*Dad: You're right; I did do that last night. That was rude, and I am sorry.
Will you please forgive me? Can we talk about your license now?*

Message: My dad cares about what is important to me.

Scripture emphasizes the importance of being teachable:

- Proverbs 12:1 — Whoever loves discipline loves knowledge, but he who hates reproof is stupid.
- Proverbs 13:18 — Poverty and shame will come to him who neglects discipline, but he who regards reproof will be honored.
- Proverbs 15:31-32 — The ear that listens to life-giving reproof will dwell among the wise. Whoever ignores instruction despises himself, but he who listens to reproof gains intelligence. (ESV)

It will be difficult to care for our daughters' hearts if we are not open to observations from them. Yes, we need to train our daughters to be thoughtful and respectful when they communicate with us, but we need to be intentional about looking to see the truth in what they are saying. If we push back when our daughters share something, they will begin to shut down. Let's make sure that our daughters know they can bring us concerns any time. And let's communicate this to them by genuinely thanking them the next time they share an observation.

Where Do I Go from Here?

As you read this chapter, you may feel convicted about things you have not done well with your daughter. Don't try to brush the conviction aside. Instead go to God and pray through what you are feeling and repent where needed. You may also need to go to your daughter and ask for forgiveness. This can prove to be a wonderful time of restoration and renewal in the relationship. Without seeking forgiveness for sin, we leave our children feeling discouraged and tempted toward bitterness. But when we repent, we take responsibility and contribute to the healing of their hearts and the strengthening of our relationship with them.

Dads, let's be honest. We start out with our daughters' hearts.
They're ours to keep... or ours to lose.

When our daughters are little, they want to be with us. We are their knights in shining armor. When they think of getting married, they want to find a husband just like us. So if we discover that we no longer have our daughter's heart, we can't blame the boy down the street or her friends or anyone else for that matter. Somewhere along the way we lost her heart. We dropped the ball. Don't make excuses, don't deny your responsibility, and don't forfeit the grace that could be yours. Instead, repent and ask God to empower you to win back her heart. She is worth it!

Prayer

Heavenly Father, help me to care for my daughter's heart.
Help me to enter her world and draw her into my world. Show
me how to communicate to her that she is beautiful and worth
fighting for. Let Your love that is within me overflow to her
every day. In all my interactions with my daughter, I want her
to see glimpses of You, her heavenly Father.

---

[1] John Eldredge and Stasi Eldredge, *Captivating* (Nashville: Thomas Nelson, Inc., 2005), 106.

[2] Dr. Alan Francis, *Everything Men Know About Women* (Riverside, CA: Andrews McMeel Publishing, 1995).

[3] Grace Mally, *Will Our Generation Speak?* (Cedar Rapids, IA: Tomorrow's Forefathers, Inc., 2012).

The Daughters Speak

Becky Says...

My absolute favorite day EVER was August 1, 2013. I rode horseback through the swamps of Florida, got lost in a forest fire, rode bareback across a river, picked blueberries, and galloped across open fields. It was AWESOME!!! And the best part was that I was able to spend it with my favorite person...my dad!

Now, some of you dads reading this are probably like, "I wish my daughter would say that she loved spending the day with me." But the truth is, we have a great relationship because of my dad, not because of me.

Maybe you're thinking, "Becky probably just has a wonderful personality that really clicks with Rich's personality." That is true! I do have a wonderful personality (I get my humility from my dad). But I also have three sisters and *all* of us have completely different personalities, and *all* of us love spending time with our dad!

I wasn't exactly the easiest child to raise. I most certainly gave my parents a run for their money. Now I am not saying that a daughter has nothing to do with having a good relationship with her dad, but I would say in the case with my dad, he has definitely played the larger role in keeping a good relationship with me.

So my encouragement to dads is to really reach out to your daughter and spend time with her! Learn what she likes and what she doesn't like. Take her on fun dates. Show her you love her and want to be there for her. And the times she draws back and doesn't return your love, keep loving her. She will remember it forever. Be the type of dad who is going to love her no matter what!

4

Stay Away From My Girl!

Protecting Your Daughter

Your daughter is handed to you for the first time. Your arms intuitively flex to hold her securely, yet your touch is gentle. You stare at her face, a miracle of exquisite detail, and you marvel at the love and responsibility that sweeps over you. You have a car seat with safety harnesses, a baby sling to keep her close, a stroller to introduce her to the world yet shield her from the elements of nature, and clothes to keep her warm. Most of all, though, you will hold her in your arms, providing a comfortable, warm, and secure cradle.

What would you do if a stranger walked in and tried to rip your daughter out of your arms? What would you do if someone came over and slapped your baby? What would you do if a friend came by, pulled back your daughter's blanket, and declared, "Wow, that is one ugly girl!"? What would you do if a woman wearing a modern business suit strode over to your child, took one look, shook her head slowly, and leaned down to whisper to your daughter, "You will never be anyone important"? What would you do if a young man sauntered in, grabbing at his crotch as he walked, looked over your little girl, nodded, and said, "Can't wait 'til this one grows up"? What would you do?

For most of us, mothers or fathers, we would respond instantly. We would tighten our hold, we would turn to shield our little girl, we would whisper beautiful truths in her ears, and we might even attack the intruder. No matter what our specific response, the message would be the same: Stay away from my girl!

God places that protectiveness in us from the very beginning. We don't need to study, we don't need counsel, and we don't need to get pumped up. We just know to protect our daughters.

For most of us, that desire to protect, that confidence to protect, fades with time. Why is that? Is it because after a careful study of Scripture we see that we are not to protect our daughters, that guarding our daughters is not an accurate reflection of God's heart? Do we pray together as parents and conclude that the best thing we can do for our daughters is to throw them in the deep end of the world's pool and hope that they will learn to swim? Do we look at girls in movies, magazines, schools, and our churches, and conclude that left to themselves, girls will turn out just fine, that the odds are in their favor? Do we look at the men in our society and see a culture of respect for women in their homes, in their music, on their websites? Do we really look at God's Word and the world around us and logically conclude that our daughters no longer need to be protected?

Why Don't We Protect Our Daughters Anymore?

Where are those protective arms when our daughter is five…eleven… fifteen? What makes our arms hang limp instead of opening up to give a comforting embrace? What makes us cross our arms over our chests instead of wrapping them around our wounded girl? And what keeps our hands occupied instead of clenching them into fists and fighting our daughter's enemy? What happens?

We Are Intimidated

I (Mary Lou) sat in the chair with Stephanie on my lap. I looked up at my pediatrician who leaned against the examining table, clipboard in hand, as he slowly, as if speaking to a kindergartner, explained why I needed to start potty training Stephanie right now because she was already eighteen months old. He confidently explained the procedure I needed to use and the importance of implementing this fail-proof method immediately.

I listened to this man, who was about ten years younger than I was, and ran through my mind pictures of my three older daughters that I had successfully potty-trained without the help of this "breakthrough" method.

Finally, I looked up at him and asked, "Do you have any children?" He hesitated a moment and then said that he had a daughter.

"How old is she?" I asked.

"Two," was his reply.

"Is she potty-trained?" I asked.

Silence. "No," he admitted. He then went on to quickly share about his wife's busy schedule and how it just hadn't been the right time yet.

"Yeah, I understand," was my only reply.

He didn't mention potty-training again.

There is a growing message in the world that "authorities" are the ones that know what's best for our children. Really? Are they wiser? Proverbs 9:10a says, "The fear of the Lord is the beginning of wisdom." Do these "authorities" fear the Lord? Is their counsel based on Scripture?

What are we to do then? Reject every word of advice unless it's a direct quote from Scripture? No, we want to be humble parents that learn from others and value their input. But valuing input is not the same as blindly following it because we are intimidated into believing that people with specific degrees know better than we do.

Our girls are gifts to *us*. We can have the confidence that God will guide us in raising His girls and that He will give us wisdom as we seek it (James 1:5). Remember, we will be the ones accountable to Him for how our daughters are raised. Many times, God uses "authorities" to help us raise physically, spiritually, and emotionally strong young ladies. But we should not have a spirit of timidity when interacting with professionals and assume they know better than we do.

All advice, no matter where it comes from, needs to be checked against the truths of Scripture, and we should seek input from wise adults who are bearing good fruit (Matt. 7:20). We need to protect our daughters, and our homes, from worldly philosophies. Look at the warning in Colossians 2:8: "See to it that no one takes you captive through philosophy and empty deception, according to the tradition of men, according to the elementary principles of the world, rather than according to Christ." Let's not be taken captive!

We Believe All Children Should Reach the Same Milestones at the Same Age

We are taught that there are perfect ages for milestones in our daughters' lives: an age to potty-train, an age to learn to read, an age to learn about sex, an age to drive, and an age to enter college. We, as parents, are expected to follow these criteria and train and release our daughters accordingly.

But we know that each girl has a different personality, a different set of strengths and weaknesses, and a different maturity rate.

Brittany is a bright, responsible, and self-motivated girl. When we heard of an afternoon enrichment school looking for a dance teacher to develop and teach classes, we encouraged her to apply. She was only fifteen, but Brittany got the job and successfully ran the dance program for years. She taught herself sign language and was soon interpreting at our Sunday church services. When she was only thirteen, she took her elderly grandmother to New York City. She was trustworthy and gifted, so we did not let age limit her experiences.

But, Brittany also struggled with pride, which showed up strongly as we were teaching her to drive. We let her get her learner's license at the minimum age allowed in our state: fifteen. As we worked to instruct her in driving, a pattern began to develop: she was never at fault when she made a mistake, and she consistently did not follow our suggestions. We prayed regularly and brought these observations to her, but the pride continued.

One day, she took her dad driving and they parked at the store. Brittany got out of the car, locked the doors, and started walking away – while the car was still running! When Rich pointed this out, Brittany insisted it was his fault because he had given her a new set of keys.

We knew we had a problem.

God opposes the proud. This is sad enough, but to be opposed while driving a three-thousand-pound vehicle that can endanger your life and the lives of others is even more intense. So, although we had helped Brittany do many things beyond her years, we held back her license and would not let her get it at sixteen when our state allowed it. Instead, we eventually let her get it when she was about 17½.

Our culture is constantly shifting and changing. For example, when we went to school, we were expected to listen to the teacher and do our assignments, or punishment would ensue. Today, teachers often need to use bribes to motivate their students to pay attention in class and complete their homework. Children have not changed; the expectations have.

In the book *Do Hard Things*, teenage authors Alex and Brett Harris say this: "Society doesn't expect much of anything from young people during their teen years—except trouble. And it certainly doesn't expect competence, maturity, or productivity. The saddest part is that, as the culture around them has come to expect less and less, young people have dropped to meet those lower expectations."[1]

Have you heard this from your daughter? *Everybody* is getting pierced, having slumber parties, wearing make-up, or going to the party. In the book *The Fallacy Detective* by Hans and Nathaniel Bluedorn, the authors describe this distortion of logic as a form of propaganda: "The *bandwagon* technique invites us to jump on the bandwagon and do what everybody else is doing. This technique pressures us to do something just because many other people like us are doing it."[2]

Isabel: Hey, Dad, a bunch of us from youth group are
going to the movies after church.

Dad: Sure, have fun!

Message: Dad doesn't care where I'm going as long as I'm with my youth group.

(Parent Alert: Many church kids have had their first experience with cigarettes, drugs, and "making out" with fellow youth group members. Like in every area of our lives, we must be diligent and informed of our daughters' activities. Church youth groups are not a "free-zone.")

Isabel: Hey, Dad, a bunch of us from youth group are going to the movies after church.

Dad: What movie are you going to see?

Isabel: I don't know, but all the kids are going. Some action movie; I don't remember the name.

Dad: Honey, it sounds like fun, but we need to find out what movie they're going to see so we can research it first.

Isabel: But Dad...it's the youth group. It's not going to be some satanic film!

Dad: I'm sure it's not, but we are responsible for what we see and hear. I love you very much, and I don't want you to have to be exposed to a movie that may not be good for your heart or your mind. If you want to go, call the leader and find out what movie they are going to. Then we can look it up.

Message: My dad wants to help me make wise choices about what I let into my heart and mind.

Speaking of Peer Pressure...

Let us not be deceived. Our daughters are not the only ones who fall prey to peer pressure. As parents we may be tempted to build our family guidelines on what other parents are doing instead of basing our decisions on convictions stemming from the Word of God.

There have been several nationally known leaders in the Christian community that have been exposed for duplicitous lifestyles. They taught strongly on the values and specifics of building a godly home, but their personal lives were filled with compromise and sin.

As a result, social media has been abuzz with parents that once purchased these parenting materials now questioning their own standards and the way their own households are run. There are many testimonies of parents that now feel lost and not sure how to raise their children.

Why is this? When a brother is caught in sin we should pray for him and his family. We should pray for godly sorrow that leads to repentance and for healing and restoration for all involved. We should grieve for those hurt and grieve for the damage done to the name of Christ. It is also good to take this opportunity to check our own lives and make sure we are aligned with the Lord. But should a leader's collapse destroy our parenting paradigm? *Well, that depends on how hard we were leaning on that leader.*[3]

The exhortations from Christian books, blogs, and seminars are meant to inspire and equip us for the work of parenting. The instruction should be received as directive, not prescriptive. Point us in the right direction, not prescribe for us exactly what we need to do. Examples in any book, including this one, should be viewed as illustrative to stir up our thinking and give us creative ways to apply biblical truths.

Certainly there are many clear commands from Scripture that apply to all parenting: not lying, not exasperating our children, correcting with gentleness, teaching about the Lord in all situations, using biblical forms of discipline, viewing our daughters as gifts...the list goes on. We cannot ignore the clear teachings of Scripture and expect God's blessing on our parenting.

But the manner in which we implement these truths will vary in each family based on family dynamics, seasons of life, personalities, and maturity. Our family culture needs to be built on convictions that spring from the Word of God and applied creatively by the leading of the Holy Spirit through our God-given personalities. Where we can go wrong is when we try to follow the way a leader is raising his family instead of being inspired and building our own convictions. *Let's stand on Scripture, not lean on man.*

If the falling of a Christian leader exposes areas in your life and parenting where you have relied on his teaching instead of relying on the Word of God, then there's one thing to do: Repent! Repent to the Lord, talk with your spouse, and repent to your children for the ways you have misled them. God opposes the proud but gives grace to the humble, and He can help you rebuild your family on biblical truths.

They Say It's Okay

Who is this mysterious "they"? It usually refers to a committee that has unanimously approved something for our daughters. A group of strangers who may, or may not, embrace the same biblical convictions that we do.

Let's say a stranger comes to my door and hands me a movie. "I've watched this and it is fine for your daughter to see," he informs me. "Pay me money, and then your daughter can sit and relax and take it all in."

"Thank you," I reply excitedly as I open my wallet, give out whatever dollar amount is expected, and then call for my daughter to hurry and see this great movie...NOT! As parents, we would probably never act like this, yet this is in essence what we are doing when we allow our daughters to go to movies based solely on their ratings.

Have you considered the plot of most movies geared toward our daughters? Two main themes arise: girl dates dangerous boy, falls in love, and everything turns out fine. Or parent says no to daughter, daughter disobeys, parents end up realizing daughter was right. Is this what we want to teach our daughters?

What about the music our daughters listen to? If our daughter has the radio on in her room, basically someone we don't know, that doesn't care anything about our daughter, has decided these are the lyrics and messages to be pumped into her brain and heart. These songs will cultivate desires in her and help form her self-image and worldview. Everyone knows how easily songs are remembered. You know when you hear a song from your teen years, how quickly you start to sing along. Songs are a powerful medium; let's make sure the music they listen to is empowering our daughters in the Lord, not suffocating them with the empty and destructive philosophies of the world.

My Daughter's A Teenager—There's Nothing I Can Do

Our daughters are growing up in a culture that caters to them. Marketers know the power that American teenagers wield over families and therefore commercials and advertising campaigns are directed at them. Teenagers are encouraged to live for today, go for the gusto, and live independently. They are encouraged to go to their teachers, counselors, or coaches for advice.

Our daughters may also expect the freedoms of an adult life without an equal increase in responsibility. *I should have spending money, choose my own friends, my own clothes, my own activities just like an adult, but not work or serve others like an adult.*

We can feel lost as parents —bombarded on all sides and tempted to throw our hands up in surrender.

Wait a minute! When we feel like this, an alarm should go off in our spirits. Something is wrong. Our arms are to nurture, direct, protect—not throw up in frustration. *We are to be led by the Holy Spirit, not driven by our culture.*

The attack on our parenting really hits hard when our daughters turn eighteen. Our lawmakers have decided that at this age, our daughters are adults. Does a girl really go to bed on the last day of her seventeenth year a child and wake up on her eighteenth birthday mature and suddenly ready to handle more responsibilities and freedoms? Our daughters may be suddenly recognized as adults in our legal system, but should our parenting abruptly change too?

Going back to our original picture of holding and caring for our daughters, why would our hands be off instead of actively guiding and directing? Yes, our parenting changes as our daughters mature and we transition from basic instruction to discipling. But don't we want to nurture and train our daughters in all seasons of her life with us? Shouldn't maturity determine freedoms, not age? There are many sixteen-year-olds that can handle situations better than some twenty-year-olds. Instead of randomly throwing our daughters into new environments based on the fact that our government considers them adults, we need to know our daughters' unique strengths and weaknesses so we can help them grow and embrace new experiences with wisdom and skill.

What about Bible times? Many say a child was considered an adult at age thirteen during this period of history. Well, let's look at what the Bible reveals about a parent's relationship with an older child.

Proverbs is called the book of wisdom. As we read it, we discover that Proverbs was written by King Solomon to his son. The wording and content of Proverbs makes it clear that it is not written to a young child but to a child that is at least as old as what Americans would consider a teenager or young adult.

What does this man, the wisest of all men, say to his son? He encourages his son to hear his father's instruction and not forsake his mother's teaching (1:8), to not be enticed by sinners (1:10), to receive his father's sayings (2:1), to hear the instructions of his father (4:1), to give attention to his father's wisdom (5:1). And how old is the son? Apparently pretty old because in Chapter 5, King Solomon encourages this son to drink from his own cistern and warns against going to an adulteress.

These are not the words of a father with a hands-off approach. His advice is covering the gamut of his son's life, even into marriage. And he pleads with his son to adhere to his advice.

Let's take a look at another example from Scripture. In Deuteronomy 21:18-21, the Old Testament response to a rebellious son is detailed: "If a man has a stubborn and rebellious son who will not obey his father or his mother," the mother and father are commanded to bring him to the elders to be punished. What do we learn? The mother and father were responsible for their son, involved in their son's life, and he was expected to obey them or face serious consequences. And what was the son's age? Well, look at the charges: "This son of ours is stubborn and rebellious, he will not obey us, he is a glutton and a drunkard." Clearly, this was not a little boy!

Our Daughters Don't Really Need to Be Protected

Is all this protection talk a little too much? Does your daughter even have an enemy? Look at what Scripture says: "Be of sober spirit, be on the alert. Your adversary, the devil, prowls about like a roaring lion, seeking someone to devour" (1 Peter 5:8). The devil is prowling about like a roaring lion seeking to possibly devour your daughter! We need to be on the alert and train our daughters to be on the alert too.

How might this roaring lion look? Satan is the father of lies (John 8:44), so He will try to lie to our daughters and tell them their lives have no meaning, they are not valuable, they need to look or act a certain way to be loved. He will try to isolate our daughters from wiser, older people who love them, and to create a culture where they rely on counsel from friends as immature as they.

The enemy can speak to our daughters through movies, songs, friends, teachers, YouTube videos, texts, and blogs. The enemy can try to devour our daughters through predatory boys, drugs, alcohol, physical attacks, and emotional attacks. We need to be involved in our daughters' lives and helping to set up and create situations where they will thrive, not be destroyed. These guidelines can look different based on the convictions of each family. Some families don't allow their daughters to go to sleepovers because of the excessive slander and foolish talk about boys. Some families don't allow cell phones or Facebook. Some homeschool, some parents are classroom volunteers. Each family is unique; the point is we must be intentional about protecting our daughters.

All of God's rules for us are based on blessing us and wanting the best for us. Every time we are told no in Scripture, it is because He has a better plan for us. We want to follow this model: establishing standards that will help our daughters to grow and flourish, instead of being deceived and destroyed.

Fellow parents, this section may be extremely painful. Maybe you've been involved in your daughter's life, but she was dramatically attacked—physically, emotionally, or spiritually. This brings great sorrow to the whole family and a wrestling with God and Scripture. When our daughter has suffered in this fallen world that is so far from heaven, we must cling to the Lord to heal us and to heal our daughter. We must help her walk through her pain, even as we ourselves walk through it. God's mercies are new every day (Lam. 3:23), and we rely on Him for the strength to face what each day holds.

Don't ignore the situation and hope it won't affect your daughter! Take it seriously and get your daughter the help she needs to process her pain through the truths of Scripture and to receive comfort and counsel from Christians who have helped others heal from similar pain. Surround yourselves with loving, wise, biblically strong friends, study the people in Scripture like Joseph to draw encouragement, bask in the refreshment of Psalms, and cry out to the Lord. Your daughter needs you to show her how to cling to Jesus and walk through difficult seasons. Each situation is different, but your daughter needs your love, compassion, and commitment to righting the wrongs done against her by intervening on her behalf relationally and legally, if necessary. Remember, your daughter is a precious gift from God, and she needs to be reminded of this during times of trouble. Your response can bring great healing to her!

Working Together to Protect Our Daughters

We are called to love our daughters. According to 1 Corinthians 13:7, love "always protects" (NIV). On this earth, we are the ones who love our daughters the most, and we are the ones to protect them. This is most effective when parents are unified. We need to draw from each other's strengths so that our daughters will benefit.

A man can better understand how boys think, how they view girls, common techniques they use to draw a girl in, and how to establish standards of modesty. A woman can better understand the temptations and emotional ups and downs of girlhood, and the importance of fully believing that she is fearfully and wonderfully made. In our marriage, we are each more aware of different attacks against our family, and we have borne the most fruit when we have listened and respected each other and worked together to protect our daughters and our entire family. At the end of this chapter, there is a special word of encouragement to dads.

What's the Difference between Protecting and Controlling?

We've seen that we begin by protecting our daughters against danger and that the worldly philosophies and lies from the enemy can try to erode this God-given desire. We've seen that there is a real, multi-faceted attack against our daughters, and that we are most effective when we cooperate as parents and draw from each other's strengths. But one question remains: how can we protect our daughters without being controlling?

The answer is: motive.

Proverbs 4:23 says, "Watch over your heart with all diligence, for from it flow the springs of life." And since our motives are in our hearts, they directly affect everything we do, and how God views what we say and do. "All the ways of a man are clean in his own sight, but the Lord weighs the motives" (Prov. 16:2). Very sobering. We are accountable to God for the motives behind the rules we make for our daughters.

Let's ask some questions to discover our motives. Do our rules to protect our daughters actually stem from a desire to protect ourselves—to protect our reputation, our free time, our finances, our comfort and ease? Do we make random rules without explaining the biblical principles behind them? Do we set up guardrails for our daughters because we are too lazy to teach them how to be discerning? Are questionable shows and movies playing in our home because we feel like plopping down in front of the TV and doing something mindless? Oh, examining the heart is difficult, but 1 Corinthians 11:31 says: "But if we judged ourselves rightly, we would not be judged."

Dad: Where are you going, young lady?

Nicky: To the party I told you about.

Dad: Oh no, you're not! No daughter of mine is walking out of this house looking like that. Get back upstairs and put on some real clothes. And wipe that clown make-up off your face!

Message: My dad doesn't want me to embarrass him!

Dad: Where are you going tonight?

Nicky: To the party I told you about.

Dad: I see you have a new dress. The color looks great on you, Honey, but it's just too short.

Nicky: But Dad! It's time to go.

Dad: Could you put some leggings on underneath?

Nicky: That would ruin the whole look.

Dad: Well...that's the point. That's not a good look for you. It draws attention to your legs and is just a distracting outfit.

Nicky: I have nothing else to wear.

Dad: You'll just have to put on one of your other outfits for tonight if you want to go to the party. But I tell you what. This weekend, let's go shopping and see if we can find an amazing and modest outfit!

Message: My dad wants me to dress modestly and he's willing to help.

One specific heart issue that can turn a protective parent into a controlling parent is anger. When our motives are wrong, we are more easily angered. A dad who is not getting respect from his wife may bitterly demand it from his daughter. A mother enraged in jealousy may make senseless rules for her daughter. A hotheaded parent may explode over a daughter's action one day and accept it the next. A proud parent may lash out if his authority is questioned. All of these will exasperate our daughters, as warned in Colossians 3:21. When we are daily bearing in mind that this is God's girl, we will approach situations with much more gentleness and humility.

Exposure That Equips

One of the best ways to navigate through this fallen world is through intentional exposure. The way in which we first learn about a topic—the opinions, images, and atmosphere—strongly affects the way that topic is stored in our hearts and brains. We know that if someone learns about sex through exposure to pornographic magazines, that person's understanding and actions in this area will be greatly distorted from God's original plan.

This is true for any subject, which makes our involvement in our daughters' lives even more paramount. We live in a fallen world. There is sin in our homes and sin throughout our communities. As parents, it is our responsibility to protect our daughters from unnecessary evil while also equipping them to be a compassionate light in a dark and dreary world. What is the balance between exposure and protection?

Katie and I (Mary Lou) were at the doctor's office for a CAT scan. The TV was blaring the local news as we sat in the waiting room. I was totally tuning out the noise and thinking through Katie's upcoming procedure, when suddenly the words of the broadcaster broke through my thoughts.

She was describing in detail a mother who had killed her two-year-old child and stuffed her in a suitcase.

Suddenly my senses were alert and I knew God was telling me, *Wake up*! Since we usually don't have the local news playing in our home, I realized this was the most vivid and horrific news story Katie had ever heard. I looked over at her and saw she was stunned. We quickly got up and moved to another room by the receptionist desk that had no chairs. I knew standing for the next half an hour would be difficult on my daughter's headache, but I knew having those news images inscribed in her mind would be much more damaging.

The receptionist encouraged us to go sit down. I politely told her that the news on the TV was just too gross for us to sit and listen to, so we stood and leaned against the wall. In a few minutes, a man from the back office who had overheard our conversation came up and asked us to follow him. He kindly smiled and led us to a private waiting room in the back where he handed us a remote control and told us we could watch whatever we wanted on TV. We thanked him and chose to just talk together instead. When we got home, we told Rich about the experience, and he prayed over both of us.

On the other hand, we have shown Katie, and all our children, pictures of burned and tortured aborted babies. They have seen pictures of children rummaging through rubbish in Bangladesh. They have seen drunken men lying on the sidewalk and have interacted with homeless people begging on the streets. What's the difference? In all these situations, we knew God had placed us in a position to help and serve others, and we introduced these topics with compassion and biblical insight. We did it on purpose because there was a purpose.

One day we got a frantic call from a friend. Her husband had gone back on a cocaine binge, and she thought he was in one of the crack houses downtown. Rich went off to find him, then brought him home to shower and have a hot meal. Then he and Rich headed out to a motel room so Rich could help him wrestle through the night against this addiction.

This man was a friend, a funny and generous man, with a great personality when he was sober. We loved him, his wife, and his children.

They were in trouble, we could help, and so we needed to expose our children. It was a great opportunity to teach our children to love while still calling out the sin in someone's life.

We talked out how this man did not just wake up one day and decide he wanted to destroy his life and his family. We discussed how sin starts small, and if it is not stopped, will always continue to grow and destroy. Sin is never stagnant. We talked about how the sin of one person affects everyone around them as we comforted his wife and watched his children struggle. We prayed hard for our friend to fully know the love of God and repent from this lifestyle.

This incident exposed our children to much, but because we were actively involved and bringing God's Word to bear on the situation, this incident blossomed compassion and a deeper understanding of the need for Christ in all of our lives. It was exposure that equipped.

How to Protect Our Daughters...Forever

We will not always be with our daughters, and they will face more and more challenges as they grow older. The best way to protect them for life is this: teach them to have a biblical worldview—and that is what all our rules along the way have been leading up to. As we have established guidelines throughout their lives, explained the biblical principles behind them, and expected obedience, we have been training our daughters to not just trust and obey us, but to ultimately trust and obey God.

When Brittany was around eleven, she got tired of listening to the Christian music we owned and wanted to listen to rock music instead. Rich grew up listening to secular rock music and knew the damage it can cause to the desires of the heart. (It's funny, we expect worship music to lift up our daughter's hearts, but somehow think ungodly lyrics are not going to weigh down their hearts.) So he established that primarily Christian music would be played in our home.

So I asked around and researched on the Internet to find Christian rock music. (I know much can be said on this topic and your specific convictions may differ. That's fine. The encouragement here is to just make sure your rules are based on biblical convictions.) We looked at various groups and their lyrics, analyzed them against Scripture, and found some great groups with some powerful messages.

Truthfully, this was fairly fun for me because I too prefer rock music. When Katie came along, it was a different story: she likes hip-hop. I was a teenager in the 80's. Rock? Yes. Hip-Hop? I don't think so. But…my preferences cannot direct my parenting. So now I too listen to Christian hip-hop and rap fairly often and have been to a couple of rap concerts that I totally enjoyed. This, though, came after examining the lyrics with my daughters.

Recently a hip-hop group that we supported came out with a new CD. While researching their new songs, Katie called me over to the computer.

"Mom, check out these lyrics. They just don't seem right. It's like they're saying, 'Look at me while I strut on the dance floor.' I don't think this is a good song for me to listen to."

Yes! God's Word trumps preferences! Katie had grown up examining song lyrics (and movies and books and conversations) to discover the worldview, and now she was taking the initiative. As we engage with our daughters in relevant conversations about the world around them and fill them with the truth of Scripture, they too can begin to develop biblical convictions that they will carry with them wherever they go.

Madison: Mom, look at this great plaque
I bought at the garage sale next door!

Mom: That rainbow is beautiful. "You are never given a dream
without also being given the power to make it come true."
Great. The hammer and nails are in the garage.

Message: I can put whatever I want on my wall.

Madison: Mom, look at this great plaque
I bought at the garage sale next door!

Mom: That rainbow is beautiful. "You are never given a dream
without also being given the power to make it come true."
Do you think that's true?

Madison: Yeah, I've heard it before.

Mom: But is it true? Any dream we want we have the power to make
it come true? What does God say about our dreams and desires?
He will give us the desires of our heart if we do what?

Madison: Delight ourselves in Him.

Mom: See that's different than what this plaque is proclaiming. That
quote is just setting you up for disappointment. We need to be reminded
to delight ourselves in Him, not feed the lie that we have the power to do
anything we want. Our excitement for our future can come from the solid
truth that we are delighting ourselves in the Lord and He loves us and will
fulfill our desires in greater ways than we could ever imagine.

Madison: Like the verse I'm memorizing: 1 Corinthians 2:9: "However, as
it is written: 'No eye has seen, no ear has heard, no mind has conceived
what God has prepared for those who love him" (NIV).

Message: Mom wants me to delight myself in the Lord and dream with
confidence based on the truth of His Word.

Let's hold our daughters closely, protect them from their enemy that seeks to destroy them, help expose the lies of Satan, while all the time pointing them to the God who loves them, who can always be trusted. May our daughters know that they are God's Girls, and they are valuable and worth protecting!

Prayer

Lord, help me to protect my daughter. May I not be deceived by the counsel of the world on what is best for her, but may I know how to best equip her for the work that You have called her to do. May she see my protection of her as an expression of Your love.

Dad to Dad

I think the greatest challenge dads face in protecting our daughters is passivity. It is a silent destroyer! We often fail to take action when a situation demands a response from us. Passivity has its roots in laziness, lack of love, and fear of man.

Passivity allowed Adam to stand quietly next to his wife while Satan deceived her, and it is what allows us as Christians to sit quietly in our pews while millions of babies are murdered at abortion mills or the poor starve in our own cities. And passivity is what allows us to remain silent when our daughters are either under attack or doing something that is destructive to their souls.

The Starting Point: An Honest Assessment

Would you consider yourself a passive father? Let's look at a few questions and see:

- If someone says something unkind to your daughter, do you step in to defend her?

- If you know your daughter has friends who are having a bad influence on her, do you help steer her away from those relationships?
- If your daughter wants to dress immodestly, watch ungodly movies, listen to ungodly music, or make other destructive decisions, do you speak up and help her see the danger of her choices?
- Are you willing to protect your daughter by saying "no" to those things that are harmful to her even though "all her friends are doing it?"
- Do you seek God for a plan to use your time wisely with your daughters or do you just go with the flow? Spontaneity is great, but sometimes it is just a reflection of a lazy heart that is unwilling to think through what is best and take action.
- Do you regularly spend time with your daughters to find out how they are doing spiritually and how they are processing different situations? This can be one of the ways that we discover where they need to be protected.

Passivity Brings Regret

For me, passivity is my greatest regret as a dad. Because I tend to be outgoing and evangelistic, I was able to easily deceive myself into thinking that I was not passive. When my wife would bring to my attention examples of passivity (Honey, why did you let our daughter slam her door?) I would point out to my wife that *she* was overreacting. The problem was not me—the problem was that my wife was just overly sensitive or overly critical. This went on for years until God used a situation with our daughter, Becky, to open my eyes.

Someone of influence had regularly criticized Becky, but I did nothing about it. I justified this by saying that the critical comments, if spoken to me, would not have bothered me. In my mind there was no problem. How wrong I was! The critical comments eventually subsided but it was only after Becky had emotionally withdrawn from both this person and us (her family).

It was apparent during this season that Becky was struggling. I spoke with her, but this did not help. I prayed and fasted for her, but did not see any breakthroughs. In a moment of desperation, I called an older friend that I had gone to in the past for parenting direction. I described what was happening and he suggested that I call a friend of his that was a pastor in my town. He described this pastor as "the most discerning person I know."

I called the pastor and he agreed to meet with me, Mary Lou, and Becky. I was glad because I saw how much Becky needed help; little did I realize how much help I needed as well. Through this pastor's counsel and input from my wife, God began the process of opening my eyes to see my failure to protect Becky. The full force of my passivity began to sink in. I had not been the shepherd God had called me to be. My lack of compassion and lack of courage had provided an open door to the enemy to come in and attempt to "steal and kill and destroy" (John 10:10).

As God convicted me of my passivity, I took Becky out on a date and confessed my sin to her. Through sobbing tears of repentance, I asked her to forgive me for failing to protect her from critical, harsh words. She graciously forgave me, and God began the process of healing our relationship. Through this, coupled with an extended time of prayer and outstanding pastoral counsel, Becky began to blossom. And by God's grace our relationship has been restored, and we both love spending time together.

How I wish I could go back and rewrite history. How I wish I could erase the pain Becky experienced from my passivity. But, sadly, I cannot. My hope in writing on this topic is twofold; 1) to encourage you to take action now to put to death passivity, and 2) to give you hope that God can restore that which we have broken through our sin.

How Do I Kill Passivity?

What can we do if we see areas of passivity in our lives? First, we need to make no excuses, call it sin, and repent. Passivity is sin? James 4:17 is clear: "Therefore, to one who knows the right thing to do and does not do it, to him it is sin."

The hardest thing about putting to death passivity is...passivity! When we are passive, we are unmotivated to take action. And when we are unmotivated to take action, we don't take action. Hence the problem!

We must recognize that the problem is likely far bigger than we realize and will take much more effort than we can muster alone. We need God's help. First John 5:14-15 says, "This is the confidence which we have before Him, that, if we ask anything according to His will, He hears us. And if we know that He hears us in whatever we ask, we know that we have the requests which we have asked from Him." Is asking God to help us put to death passivity in accordance with His will? Absolutely! Therefore, we should ask for God's help and be confident that He will give us what we ask.

We also need our brothers in Christ to come alongside us and hold us accountable to take action. Sometimes it is easy to confess a sin and talk about how wrong it is, but it is not always as easy to make tangible changes. Why is that? Because sin is so deceptive. We think that because we named our sin and confessed it to others that we have changed; but we haven't changed at all until we...change! Hebrews 3:13 says, "But exhort one another daily, while it is called 'Today,' lest any of you be hardened through the deceitfulness of sin" (NKJV). We need fellow Christians to exhort us to press on and not be hardened by the deceitfulness of sin.

It is also helpful to recognize the consequences of continuing to remain passive. Proverbs 1:32-33 says, "For the waywardness of the naive will kill them, and the complacency of fools will destroy them. But he who listens to me shall live securely and will be at ease from the dread of evil."

Sometimes Christians forget that there are consequences for our actions. We think that because we have been reconciled to God through Jesus Christ, we are exempt from God's chastisement. But the principle of sowing and reaping in Scripture applies to all of us. If we continue to sow things that are displeasing to God, we will reap the consequences—and so will our daughters.

Lastly, we can meditate on scriptures that clearly reveal the opposite of passivity:

- Proverbs 21:5 — The plans of the diligent lead surely to abundance, but everyone who is hasty comes only to poverty. (ESV)
- Romans 12:9-11 — Let love be genuine. Abhor what is evil; hold fast to what is good. Love one another with brotherly affection. Outdo one another in showing honor. Do not be slothful in zeal, be fervent in spirit, serve the Lord. (ESV)
- Joshua 1:9 — Have I not commanded you? Be strong and courageous. Do not be frightened, and do not be dismayed, for the Lord your God is with you wherever you go. (ESV)

Dad, if you are feeling the conviction of the Holy Spirit, be courageous. Where you have sinned and hurt your daughter through passivity, go to her and repent. It is never too late. God is a God of restoration and can turn the heart of your daughter back to you. Pray, fast, repent. Do this for your daughter because she is worth fighting for! It's time for us to rise up as men and put to death passivity. Let's not let this insidious enemy destroy our relationship with our daughters.

Deeds of Repentance

My daughter, Becky, expressed concern about a suspicious looking customer that came into the bookstore where she worked. The man came in the store around closing time, did not seem interested in any of the books at the store, and was acting in an unusual manner. Then she saw this same person at a nearby restaurant a couple days later. Her concern was that he would come back to the store the next time she worked the closing shift. Because of the way they locked the building, she would be going out back at night in a dark isolated area.

When she shared this with me, I immediately told her that her brothers and I would go to the store to protect her the next time she closed. Now, what her brothers lacked in size (they were eight, eleven, and thirteen years old at the time), they made up for in passion. They were all eager to go protect Becky and capture the "bad guy." So the next night Becky worked, we all headed up to the store and got there about twenty minutes before closing time. We cased the entire retail center, making note of any suspicious looking vehicles or people. The boys were convinced that the guy smoking in the back parking lot was a gun-toting gang member.

The suspicious guy Becky had seen did not show up, and we did not need to make a citizen's arrest of the smoker in the back. Uneventful in one sense, but a powerful message to Becky that her dad and brothers care about her and want to protect her, and that her dad was serious about putting to death passivity.

Pray for Her

One of the primary ways you can protect your daughter is by praying for her. Not methodical prayers on the drive to work, where we rattle off the same requests every day without thinking. Instead, passionate faith-filled prayers that please the Lord.

A great passage on prayer is Colossians 4:12, "Epaphras, who is one of you and a servant of Christ Jesus, sends greetings. He is always wrestling in prayer for you, that you may stand firm in all the will of God, mature and fully assured" (NIV).

Let the full force of this passage sink in. Epaphras wasn't occasionally praying for the church at Colossae. He wasn't daily lifting up a rote prayer list. He was *always wrestling in prayer* for them. Epaphras was a man who was energized by the desire to see his brothers and sisters be all they could be in the Lord—and it drove him to intense prayer.

Don't we want the same thing for our daughters? Then let us be like Epaphras—always wrestling in prayer for our daughters that they may stand firm in all the will of God, mature and fully assured.

Maybe at this point you might say your prayers have not been intense. How can we move from perfunctory prayer to passionate prayer? In Luke 11:1, the disciples asked Jesus to teach them to pray. Jesus taught them what is referred to as the "Lord's Prayer" and then went on to share the following parable with them in verses 5-9:

Then He [Jesus] said to them, "Suppose one of you has a friend, and goes to him at midnight and says to him, 'Friend, lend me three loaves; for a friend of mine has come to me from a journey, and I have nothing to set before him'; and from inside he answers and says, 'Do not bother me; the door has already been shut and my children and I are in bed; I cannot get up and give you anything.' I tell you, even though he will not get up and give him anything because he is his friend, yet because of his persistence he will get up and give him as much as he needs. So I say to you, ask, and it will be given to you; seek, and you will find; knock, and it will be opened to you."

What an incredible truth! The man in the parable has nothing to give his friend, yet he knows his neighbor has what his friend needs. And though his neighbor's initial response is a flat out refusal, the man is not daunted. He remains bold and does not give up until he gets what he needs for his friend.

At first you might think, shouldn't he have accepted no for an answer? Isn't he being pushy and presumptuous? That certainly is not God's perspective. *God commends the man for his persistence and grants his request.*

This is an excellent model for intercession. We don't always have what our daughters need. We don't always know the right questions to ask or the right things to say. But we can go to God and ask Him to meet their needs and ask Him to equip us to parent our daughters well. God has what we all need.

Why Is God Not Answering My Prayer?

Before leaving the topic of prayer, we should consider one of the primary reasons God does not answer prayer. Psalm 66:18 says, "If I had cherished sin in my heart, the Lord would not have listened" (NIV). The

Lord tells us very plainly in this verse that we should not expect an answer to prayer if we hold on to sin, if we refuse to repent. There are innumerable sins that we could hold on to, but let's look at three that can be major obstacles in our prayer life:

1) Pride

   James 4:6 says God opposes the proud but gives grace to the humble. How do you know if you are a proud person? Here are some "pride revealing" questions:

   a. How do you respond when someone brings you correction? Are you teachable?
   b. Do you listen when others are talking and ask them relevant questions about what they shared, or do you just want to talk about yourself?
   c. Do you make sure you are recognized and honored?
   d. Do you think you are better than others?
   e. Do you regularly seek God when making decisions, or do you rely on your own wisdom?

   We must choose to humble ourselves if we want God to lift us up. If we do not do this, God will oppose us.

2) Unforgiveness/Bitterness

   Matthew 18:32-35 says,

   Then summoning him, his lord said to him, "You wicked slave, I forgave you all that debt because you pleaded with me. Should you not also have had mercy on your fellow slave, in the same way that I had mercy on you?" And his lord, moved with anger, handed him over to the torturers until he should repay all that was owed him. My heavenly

Father will also do the same to you, if each of you does not forgive his brother from your heart.

This is one of the scariest verses in the Bible. God will turn us over to the torturers if we fail to forgive! Hebrews 12:15 says, "See to it that no one misses the grace of God and that no bitter root grows up to cause trouble and defile many" (NIV). Not only will God not answer our prayers when we remain bitter and unforgiving, but we will defile others in the process.

3) Not living with your wife in an understanding manner

1 Peter 3:7 says,

Husbands, in the same way be considerate as you live with your wives, and treat them with respect as the weaker partner and as heirs with you of the gracious gift of life, so that nothing will hinder your prayer. (NIV)

Here is yet another verse where we see God explicitly telling us that our prayers will be hindered by sin. In this case the sin is not living with our wives in a considerate manner and treating them with respect. Perhaps you are not sure if you are living with your wife in an understanding manner. Here is an easy way to find out: ask your wife!

Ultimately, there is GREAT hope in discovering that our sin has kept God from answering our prayers! It should bring joy to our hearts, because then we can do something about it. First John 1:9 says, "If we confess our sins, He is faithful and righteous to forgive us our sins and to cleanse us from all unrighteousness." Where pride, unforgiveness, not being considerate as a husband, or some other sin has caused God to not listen to our prayers, there is one prayer that God always hears—the prayer of repentance! God will give grace to the humble.

Press On

Some may say the Lord has not given what you asked for because it is not His will. But don't just assume this is the case if at first God does not answer. The neighbor did not assume this and he got what he was seeking. Even Paul, when asking the Lord to remove the thorn from his flesh did not stop asking until God specifically revealed to him that His grace was sufficient (2 Cor. 12:9).

So let us press on with our requests for our daughters. Let us not give up if at first there is no answer. Let us recognize that Scripture is replete with exhortations to pray in faith, believing that we will receive what we ask. And let us not forget that when we pray for our daughters, we are praying to their heavenly Father who loves them far more than we ever could.

Prayer for Dads

Lord, help me to honestly assess myself and see where I have allowed passivity in my life. Forgive me for being passive and help me to walk in deeds of repentance. Let me not allow passivity or any other sin to hinder my prayers. May I be a father who wrestles in prayer regularly for my daughter, that she may stand firm in Your will, mature and fully assured.

---

[1] Alex Harris and Brett Harris, *Do Hard Things* (Colorado Springs: Multnomah Books, 2008) 36.
[2] Nathaniel Bluedorn and Hans Bluedorn, *The Fallacy Detective* (Muscatine, IA: Christian Logic, 2009) 159.
[3] For help in walking your daughter through the public downfall of a Christian leader, check out this article at www.raisingrealmen.com: "How to Talk to Your Children When Christian Leaders Fall."

RAISING GOD'S GIRL

The Daughters Speak

Brittany Says...

My dad really hit on the power of confession and asking for forgiveness in this chapter. This can speak volumes to your daughters. I remember times growing up when each of my parents confessed sin to us and asked for our forgiveness. While restoration with those you have sinned against is extremely important, there were actually other confessions from my parents that had a much bigger impact.

When my parents repented for sins they had committed against us, it was either expected, like we all kind of knew they had messed up, or it was completely unexpected and we didn't even realize they had done anything wrong. However, what affected me even more was when they repented of sins that *we* pointed out to them—even about areas that had nothing to do with us. I was always very impressed when my parents would take what we had said to heart and then follow up and tell us what God had revealed to them. This made us feel like our voices were being heard. We were treated as Christians who hear from God and not looked down upon or ignored because of our youth.

The other type of confession that had a big impact was when they would confess sin to us from their personal lives. This could be specific examples of where they were convicted of speaking unkindly to a friend or a more general confession of how they had been struggling with unkindness in their marriage. We knew that they had no obligation to tell us, but they did so out of humility and openness. That set an example for us to be open about failures and to give God glory when He helps us see sin and change.

Another thing my dad mentioned was always protecting us daughters. This is something that both moms and dads can, and should, do. My mom always listened to us about any and every concern we had. She never told us that our fears or problems were irrational or that we should just grow up and forget about it. She heeded whatever we had to say and would offer counsel, or if the situation was more serious, ask my dad to step in and help us. My dad was not afraid of confrontation if it was needed, and so I trusted him to always step up and protect us. This saved me from having to be in uncomfortable situations or from wasting time trying to figure everything out myself and not seeking counsel from others.

An additional way I always felt protected was by how often my parents prayed for me. I knew they prayed separately and together for me every day. There was only so much they could physically do to protect us from harm, but they knew God could do infinitely more. Instead of wasting time worrying about what they couldn't fix or change, they spent that time crying out to the One who could! I always knew wherever I went I was in their prayers and in God's hands.

GOD INTERRUPTS

Back at the local café…

Wow, our time together has been great! We've laughed together and cried together. Inspired each other and confessed our struggles to each other. Our vision for our daughters has been growing as we have been reminded afresh that they are gifts from God and need to be raised for Him.

The waitress comes over to refill our drinks, and I glance at my watch.

"I can't be out too late tonight. I've got to get up early in the morning to take my daughter to the train station. She's riding down to spend some time with her grandmother."

"What time does she need to be there?" you ask.

"The train leaves at 5:00am. It's a pretty big station and at that time of day I just hope I get her on the right train."

As the words come out of my mouth, we all stop what we're doing and look at each other. We know in this moment that God is speaking to our hearts. In all that we've discussed, embracing our daughters as gifts, building strong biblical relationships with them, and protecting and teaching them

about the world around them, we've not mentioned the most
important: helping them to get on the right train.

The truth is we only have our daughters for a short time. The years with our daughters will fly by and what will really matter, when all is said and done, is what train our daughters are on.

So let's picture this: You bring your beautiful girl to the train station. You have carefully packed her suitcase with appropriate clothes for all kinds of weather. You have checked her assigned car to make sure it's clean, talked to the passengers surrounding her seat and discovered they are all pleasant and kind. You have researched and packed only healthy, organic snacks. You even arranged for a tutor on the train to help her with her studies.

But you are a super parent. You want to go beyond just providing a comfortable journey for your daughter. You decide to run alongside the train, calling out through the open window to your daughter. Telling her how much you love her and how wonderful she is. Encouraging her that she is a gifted young woman and that she can accomplish much. Other passengers look out the window admiringly as they observe your commitment and dedication to your daughter. *That's a great parent!*

As the train moves away from the station, it suddenly rounds a bend and begins to head back towards you. As the front of the train comes closer, you look up, and across the top of the engine's window you see the train's destination written in bold letters.

Wait! Your blood pressure soars as panic whips through your body. Though your stomach is in knots, your legs begin chasing after the train, sweat pouring down your face, your heart pounding as you scream: "Wait! Stop the train! My daughter's on the wrong train! Get her off!" You run as hard as you can, with only one image in your mind, the destination written on the front of the train: Destruction.

For although it is important that we treat our daughters with kindness and provide an environment where they can thrive and feel cherished and loved, the purpose of it all is to be faithful to God and lead them to the train with a different destination: Heaven.

Truthfully, that train is not always the shiniest in the station. It shows some wear and tear both inside and out from years of rescuing people and bringing them through treacherous places. To lead your daughter to this train, you must be honest.

"Honey, the train you're getting on may go over some rough terrain. Sometimes you will go through dark tunnels that seem to never end. Other times, the train will sway back and forth as you journey through storms, and then almost crawl along as you traverse over deserts. As you ride through some towns, people will sneer at you and throw things at the train. But let me tell you: The tracks are secure, and I personally know the engineer and I trust Him fully to get you to your destination."

And then you take your daughter to meet your friend, your Lord, your Savior, the engineer of this train...Jesus.

You can only lead your daughter to this train. You cannot put her on this train; she must step into this train herself (John 1:12). But you can certainly devote yourself to teaching and encouraging her to join the multitude of other Christians on this journey.

Dear friends, we do not want to be excellent parents on earth but not prepare our daughters for eternity. As John Tillotson said, "He who provides for this life, but takes not care for eternity, is wise for a moment, but a fool forever."[1] All our sacrifices and efforts in biblical parenting are for this ultimate purpose: to illuminate to our daughters God's unfailing love, their need for a savior, His sovereignty, and His divine purposes for their lives. We want to lead our daughters to the Lord.

How do we do that?

Should we play worship music while they are in the womb? Should we pray over them as they nurse? Should we pray before meals? Should we read Bible storybooks out loud? Should we share the gospel with them no matter how old they are? Should we teach them to ask God's forgiveness when they disobey? Should we dance with our daughters and shout to the Lord in times of praise? Should we weep with our daughters and cry out to God in times of sorrow and confusion? Should we use Scripture to correct our daughters? Should we use Scripture to encourage our daughters?

The answer to all these questions is a resounding Yes! As Christians, our love for the Lord and our commitment to His Word needs to permeate our homes, our conversations, and our relationships. Some parents are tempted to approach sharing the gospel with their children like they teach sex: with a one-time, orchestrated in advance, generally awkward conversation.

No, our discussion of the gospel should be lively, invigorating, and never ending. "For God so loved the world that He gave His only begotten son. That whoever believes in Him shall not perish but have eternal life" should be lived out on the soccer field, the theater stage, the classroom, the bedroom.[2] All areas of our life should be *directed* by our trust in Christ and *reflective* of our trust in Christ. "Whether, then, you eat or drink or whatever you do, do all to the glory of God" (1 Cor. 10:31).

Does your daughter know that God loved her so much that He gave His only Son, so that if she believes in Him she will not perish, but she will have eternal life? Does she even know that she needs rescuing?

Proverbs 14:12 says, "There is a way which seems right to a man, but its end is the way of death." Does she think that because she is growing up in a Christian home that she is automatically a Christian? Does your daughter think that because she goes to church or does good to others that she will go to heaven?

The Bible says there is no one good. All have sinned and fallen short of the glory of God. Every one of us has broken God's commandments and stands guilty before a holy God. And the wages of sin is death. That means separation from God forever in hell. Our daughters need to see this. They need to understand the gravity of their predicament.

And they need to understand the power of God's love! The good news is that while we were yet sinners Christ died for us. He left the beauty of heaven and came down to earth to live among sinful man. He lived a perfect and sinless life, and then let Himself be crucified on the cross so that we can be forgiven and led to God.

God now offers us salvation from destruction and eternity with Him in heaven if we will repent and believe on the Lord Jesus.[3]

Has your daughter put her trust in the Lord?

Have you?

Let's stop right here. Children are a gift from God and one of the ways they are gifts is that they help reveal what's in our hearts. As you've been reading this, is something churning in your heart? Are you a little uncomfortable with the thought of eternity? Do you know the Savior? Do you know the One that drives the train headed for heaven? Are you having a difficult time leading your daughter to the Lord because He is not someone you know?

My friend, read no further. We have talked about wanting to be excellent parents, but there is only one perfect parent, and that is God. He is your perfect Father who is using your desire to raise your daughter well to reveal an emptiness in your own heart. Wait no longer! Repent today.

There is no formula prayer. The Lord is calling out to you today and asking you to respond. Confess to the Lord that you have sinned. Ask him to forgive you and cleanse you from all unrighteousness. Up until now you have been Lord of your own life. Turn today and make Jesus Lord of your life. He hears your prayers, He sees your heart, and He wants none to perish. "The Lord is not slow about His promise, as some count slowness, but is patient toward you, not wishing for any to perish but for all to come to repentance" (2 Peter 3:9). Receive His forgiveness today and walk in the confidence and security of being led by the hand of God Almighty.

If you've just prayed along these lines, and meant it from your heart, then rejoice! Your name is written in the book of life (Rev. 20:15), and you are on your way to heaven. Now find other believers, share with them your commitment, dive into the Bible, and obey what God says. And most of all, tell your daughter!

---

[1] John Tillotson, izquotes, accessed 1 May 2015, www.izquotes.com.

[2] John 3:16.

[3] Romans 3:10-18; Romans 3:23; Romans 6:23; Romans 5:8; 1 Peter 3:18; Acts 3:19; Acts 16:31; 1 Corinthians 15:3-5. For further reading, explore the Eternal Perspectives Ministry website (www.epm.org) and especially the article entitled, "Can You Know You're Going to Heaven?"

5

That's My Girl?

Walking through Seasons of Disappointment and Pain

I (Mary Lou) was sure Brittany was the most beautiful two-year-old God had ever created. As my only child at the time, we spent our days playing with dolls and wearing dress-up clothes. We laughed together, read the Bible together, and worked around the house together. It was a joy to spend my days with her.

At this moment, though, Brittany had disobeyed me and needed to be corrected. I wasn't daunted by the task. Rich and I had received excellent teaching on biblical parenting before we even had children. I had a vision for my purpose as a mom. I knew that I was called to reflect God's love to my daughter. I knew I was to encourage her in godly character. I knew I was to correct her sin with great faith, knowing that as she saw her sin, she would see her need for a Savior. I knew my correction was to be redemptive and restorative, with none of my affection withheld during the process or afterwards. I had prayed as we walked back to my room, and I was ready for this important aspect of parenting.

I sat Brittany down in front of me. I got down on her level and looked straight into her big, brown eyes. I clearly explained how she had disobeyed me. I waxed on eloquently about how much I loved her and how God loved her even more than I did. I reminded her that God sent Jesus to die on the cross for her sins and mine. I looked at her compassionately and told her that because I loved her, I would teach her to obey me in the Lord.

My sweet daughter stared at me intently throughout my exhortation to godliness. Then, out of the corner of my eye, I saw her chubby little hand lift up. The little hand that had clung around my finger when I nursed her as a baby. The little hand that clung to mine as we crossed the street. The little hand that now lifted higher and…slapped me across the face!

I was stunned. I had never slapped her, and Rich and I never slapped each other. Where did that come from?

Proverbs 22:15 answers this for me: "Foolishness is bound up in the heart of a child; the rod of discipline will remove it far from him." That foolishness was not learned from her parents or friends; that foolishness came from her heart.

And thus began our journey of learning the truth in that Scripture, learning that there are times that our daughters' sin comes from within—not copied from anyone. Learning that there are environments that fertilize that propensity to sin, learning that there are environments that help remove these weeds from their hearts and allow more space for beauty to blossom. Learning that an understanding of our daughters' struggles does not take away the pain of walking through them. And learning that no matter what part of the journey we are on, we need to love our daughter unconditionally each step along the way.

All seven of our children are growing in the Lord. The path, though, has not always been easy. Sometimes the difficulties came from their sin, sometimes from ours, sometimes from attacks from the enemy, sometimes as consequences of living in a fallen world, and sometimes a mixture of all four. In this chapter we will discuss some examples of difficult seasons that we can face as parents. We cannot cover every scenario, nor can we capture the unique nuances of your specific trials. But what we can do is trust the Holy Spirit to speak to us through other's struggles and victories and reveal to us how the biblical principles discussed can be applied in our own lives and families.

How Should I Respond When My Daughter Sins?

It's no wonder I am exhausted; I am surrounded by sinners all day long! And the worst part is that when I brush my teeth every morning, I look up and see the chief of sinners staring back at me from the mirror (1 Tim. 1:15). Life can be challenging, and parenting only increases the pressure and the stakes. Let's look at some biblical qualities that can help us succeed in this adventure of *Raising God's Girl*.

Compassion

A discussion on addressing sin in our daughters' lives needs to start with an exhortation to be compassionate. If my daughter was having a painful appendix attack, and I had never experienced one, I should choose to be compassionate and helpful to the best that I could. *But* if I had previously suffered an appendix attack, oh how much greater my compassion and empathy would be, how much more patient and skillful I would be in helping her.

So it is when our daughters are struggling with sin. We should be super compassionate and empathetic, filled with hopeful exhortations and practical advice. Why? Because we too are sinners and have sinned much longer than our daughters!

Mom: Teresa, come see Mommy right now, please.

Teresa stomps over with arms crossed.

Mom: Stop yelling at your sister.

Teresa: But she broke my Barbie doll.

Mom: Look, you've got a hundred other dolls.
Whatever she did, I don't want to hear you yelling.

Message: I need to make sure Mom doesn't hear me yelling.

Mom: Teresa, come see Mommy right now, please.

Teresa stomps over with arms crossed.

Mom: Honey, I see that you're mad at your sister.

*Teresa: Well, yeah. She broke the head off my
Barbie and threw it across the room.*

*Mom: I know, and I'm going to talk to her about it in a minute.
But first I want to talk with you. I know you're angry, but you are
not allowed to yell at your sister and call her a "fat head."*

Teresa: But she purposely broke my doll. And it was one of my favorites!

*Mom: I totally understand why you are upset. But that does not
allow you to disobey me and be mean to your sister.*

Teresa: But she was mean to me.

*Mom: I know, but we are talking about you right now. That feeling
you have right now is anger. When this rises up in you, I want to
help you learn to have self-control. Yelling at someone when you
are mad is called an outburst of anger. It's disobeying God and
disobeying me. When this feeling rises, you need to make the right
choice next time and tell your sister that she needs to tell me what
she did. If she doesn't, then you can come and get me. I love you,
and I want to help both of you learn how to handle conflicts well.*

Message: Mom tries to understand and wants to help.

It's difficult when someone is mean to us. It's difficult when work is hard. It's difficult when we don't get what we want. We know this, so shouldn't we be compassionate when our daughters struggle with the same things? Psalm 103:13 says, "Just as a father has compassion on his children, so the Lord has compassion on those who fear Him." God used a father's compassion to his children as an example of His own compassion! Certainly we need to demonstrate this trait to our daughters. And as we grow in compassion, our words of instruction will be much more palatable.

Let's take a look at Jesus. In Matthew 9 we read about Jesus going throughout the cities and teaching. "Seeing the people, He felt *compassion* for them, because they were distressed and dispirited like sheep without a shepherd" (v. 36, emphasis added). Surely Jesus, who was omniscient, was fully aware of the people's sins, yet He had compassion for them.

How about the story of the prodigal son who had left his family and gone off and wasted his inheritance? Luke 15:20 describes the scene when the son realizes he was wrong and returns home: "So he got up and came to his father. But while he was still a long way off, his father saw him, and felt *compassion* for him, and ran and embraced him and kissed him" (emphasis added).

No matter what stage of maturity our daughters are in, distressed and dispirited or turning in repentance, we are to follow the example of Christ and establish a culture of compassion in our home.

Conviction

Compassion for our daughters should not dampen our desire to correct them; instead compassion should strengthen our conviction to train them. "Train up a child in the way he should go, even when he is old he will not depart from it" (Prov. 22:6). Because we know how hard it is to battle sin and temptation, and because we know how hard it can be to interact with others, we are all the more motivated to instruct our daughters while they are still young and teach them biblical principles for fighting sin, growing in the Lord, and relating well with others.

What type of training should we give? Well, the entire Bible is our curriculum for life. It is the book to teach us how to avoid difficulties and the book to turn to when difficulties arise. Second Timothy 3:16-17: "All Scripture is inspired by God and profitable for teaching, for reproof, for correction, for *training* in righteousness; so that the man of God may be adequate, equipped for every good work" (emphasis added). Yes, we want our daughters trained in righteousness and equipped for every good work!

We are to use Scripture to help our daughters practice and learn from situations so they can be discerning and maturing in the Lord. "But solid food is for the mature, who because of practice have their senses *trained* to discern good and evil" (Heb. 5:14, emphasis added). Yes, we want our daughters to be able to discern between good and evil!

We are to use our authority in our daughters' lives to gently discipline them. "All discipline for the moment seems not to be joyful, but sorrowful; yet to those who have been *trained* by it, afterwards it yields the peaceful fruit of righteousness" (Heb. 12:11). Yes, we want a bountiful harvest of the peaceful fruit of righteousness in our daughters' lives!

Hailey: I saw Mrs. Young at the store today. She said Aubrey had her wisdom teeth pulled and would love some company.

Mom: What did you say to her?

Hailey: I just said, "Oh, I'm sorry to hear that." Then I rushed over to the next aisle. There's no way I'm going by to visit "little miss princess" after the way she destroyed my red dress. She borrowed it for a party and then wore it to the beach! What was she thinking? She didn't even apologize when I saw it tossed in the corner of her room.

Mom: Yeah, well, it's her loss.

Message: If someone's mean to me, then our friendship is over.

Hailey: I saw Mrs. Young at the store today. She said Aubrey
had her wisdom teeth pulled and would love some company.

Mom: What did you say to her?

Hailey: I just said, "Oh, I'm sorry to hear that." Then I rushed over to
the next aisle. There's no way I'm going by to visit "little miss princess
herself" after the way she destroyed my red dress. She borrowed it for a
party and then wore it to the beach! What was she thinking? She didn't
even apologize when I saw it tossed in the corner of her room."

Mom: I can understand how frustrating that must be.
But I wonder if there's some way you could show her kindness?
I think of that passage in Luke 6 that tells us how to treat our enemies.
I'm always challenged by this, especially verse 35: "But love
your enemies, and do good, and lend, expecting nothing in return;
and your reward will be great, and you will be sons of the Most High;
for He Himself is kind to ungrateful and evil men."

Message: I need to discover what Scripture says about my situation.

Commitment

We need to be committed parents, no matter how stormy life gets. But what are we to be committed to? We need to be committed to raising God's girls in His way, with His power—for His purposes. This sobering commitment leads to the next: We need to be committed to loving our daughters even when they are acting "unlovable." Here we are going to get into the messy part of parenting. The part that can be embarrassing and bring turmoil to the whole family. What do we do when our daughters' sin is exploding all over the place?

The answer is this: stay committed to your love for her and your desire to see her walk in all the Lord has for her. And when that commitment is honestly just not strong enough, cling to the Lord and show love to your daughter because you fear the Lord and are committed to Him.

Does this last statement shock you? That our commitment to loving our daughters might not be strong enough to get us through the storm? Or maybe you've felt that way, but never put it into words. The truth is parenting is hard, especially when our daughters are resistant.

Picture this: what if your co-worker was mad at you all the time, glared at you when you walked by, rolled her eyes when you made a suggestion, and tried to ignore you when you walked into her office to talk about something? Would you want to work with her?

What if you overheard one of your friends talking about how mean you are and stole money from your drawer whenever she was in your home? Would you want to hang out with her?

Or what if a friend stopped by for dinner and was grumpy and made fun of what was being shared during mealtime conversation? Would you want to include her in family gatherings?

The answer to these questions is no, of course not. But we are called to co-labor with our daughters, hang out with them, and include them in family events. Deuteronomy 6:6-7 teaches us: "These words, which I am commanding you today, shall be on your heart. You shall teach them diligently to your sons and shall talk of them when you sit in your house and when you walk by the way and when you lie down and when you rise up." This describes a life of hanging out with daughters, with no escape clause for difficulty.

The truth that parenting is hard is followed by another truth: parenting can hurt. We can be hurt by what our daughters do and say, and even more so because we love them so much. *The exact heart attitude that helps make us great parents also opens us up to great hurt.* When we pour our hearts into raising our daughters and give them our very best, it is devastating when this is refused, even temporarily. We can feel rejected. It is then our natural instinct to want to close up and protect ourselves—to distance ourselves from the pain and ultimately distance ourselves from our daughter.

But this is where commitment to the Lord comes to the rescue.

Cleansing

A Commitment to the Lord + A Commitment to My Daughter =
A Heart That Forgives

Because we are committed to raising our daughters in the fear of the Lord, we know we must cleanse our own hearts and forgive them. Right here, right now, while we are hurt, while our daughters are acting mean. We must forgive them.

Oh, this is a hard one.

One of our daughters went through a season of struggling with anger. Her sporadic outbursts of anger would often send us all scattering to our rooms to cope with this environment. The pressure of daily carrying our daughter in prayer, encouraging her, correcting her, helping her siblings cope, and seeking help and counsel was exhausting. I (Mary Lou) was tired of always being wrong in my daughter's eyes, never able to have a normal conversation with her and nervous all day wondering when the next outburst would erupt. Many afternoons when I went in my room for my quiet time, I just cried out to God, wanting to escape, wanting to put on my red bathrobe and sit in the corner of my room until the anger stopped. During these moments, I felt unable to think or reason clearly, and my only desire was to get out of there.

Each time I got to this place, the gentle voice of the Lord would break through. In the middle of my rambling complaints to God about all the mean things my daughter was doing, I would feel that quiet check in my spirit: "Forgive her."

"But, Lord! She's being mean to me. Mean to my other children. And she just won't stop!"

"I know. Forgive her."

And then I would know that this was no longer an issue between me and my daughter. It was now an issue between me and my Lord. He has told me what to do. Would I obey Him?

For the Lord loves me and could see what was causing my emotional breakdown and desire to flee: I was being tormented. And why was I being tormented? Because I had a daughter struggling with anger? No, I was being tormented because I had unforgiveness in my heart.

The effects of unforgiveness are very clear in Matthew 18 when Jesus teaches about a slave that owed a king quite a bit of money. The king commanded that the man and his entire family be sold for repayment of the debt. The slave begged for patience, and the king released him from his debt.

But then the slave knew another man who owed him money. When that man was unable to pay, the forgiven slave had no mercy on him and had him thrown into jail. When the king heard about this forgiven slave's refusal to forgive the debts of others, his response is recorded in verse 34: "And his lord [king], moved with anger, handed him over to the torturers until he should repay all that was owed him."

And Jesus then turns, looks at us, and says: "My heavenly Father will also do the same to you, if each of you does not forgive his brother from your heart" (v. 35).

And so I choose to obey the Lord. Today, tomorrow, and the next day I will choose to obey the Lord and forgive my daughter because I love Him, I don't want to be turned over to the tormentors, and I know forgiving my daughter brings me freedom to raise her in love and faith.

How Do I Forgive My Daughter?

How do we forgive? It's one thing to get to the point where we clearly see God's command to us in the crisis, but it's another thing to walk it out. How do we forgive our daughters?

We start with a cleansing of our own heart: "Father, please forgive me for my unforgiveness. I repent and turn from this wicked way. I desire to obey You and forgive my daughter. Please help me to do this. I forgive her in the name and power of Jesus Christ, and I release her from her debt to me."

We can forgive because we have been forgiven. The slave was forgiven by the king and then needed to turn around and forgive those who owed him…much less.

Our sin against the Lord is huge. He's seen every action, every thought, every motive! Can you imagine that? Imagine having all your sinful actions, thoughts, and motives played in a video before your church family this week. It's a horrible thought, but our Lord has forgiven us and washed us clean. So then, because we have been the recipients of such magnanimous forgiveness, we too can turn and forgive others whose sins against us pale in comparison to ours against the Almighty King. Colossians 3:13 "…forgiving each other, whoever has a complaint against anyone; just as the Lord forgave you, so also should you."

Here's an interesting note: Let's look back on the original act of forgiveness by the king in Matthew 18. Verse 27 says, "And the lord [king] of that slave felt *compassion* and released him and forgave him the debt" (emphasis added). What preceded the release? Compassion, which ties in to the point earlier in this chapter.

Our daughters are not our enemies and they should not be treated as such. The enemy is the enemy and he is messing with us and he is messing with our daughters. He is the one that we need to put up a wall against, not our daughters. We need to build a wall around us and our daughters that protects us from our enemy, not build a wall between us and our daughters that separates us. For every brick that the enemy tries to place between us and our daughters, let's pick it up, hold it up to the Lord, and declare, "I forgive my daughter and this brick is now sanctified unto the Lord. I choose to cover this in the blood of Jesus and set it in place on the fortress wall against the attack of our enemy."

Practicing True Forgiveness

Recognizing the weight of our own sin (as demonstrated in Matthew 18) and putting on a heart of compassion are beautiful tools to help us embrace a life of extending forgiveness, *but* this can sometimes lead to a hyper-spiritual paralyzing of our soul that leaves us damaged and bearing wounds in our heart that we don't understand. Seeing the magnitude of God's forgiveness to us and having compassion on our daughters does not mean we are to minimize our daughters' sins or the effects on us. How might this look?

"Well, I know Christy slammed the door on me again while I was still talking to her, but she's really under a lot of stress at work. I've behaved much worse in my life."

What's the problem with this? It leaves us in "no man's land," a gray area where we partially forgive, partially excuse. And what's the result? *By describing our daughters' sin against us as small, we only forgive something small.* Well, that's nice, *but what about the huge hurt that's in our hearts from their actions?* It's left there to grow and fester into bitterness. And regretfully that bitterness will come out in some other action or attitude that completely surprises us and leaves us wondering why we are struggling with our feelings for our daughters. Another brick in the wall between us.

Instead let's call our daughters' sins what they are: hurtful. Let's truthfully acknowledge their actions and the results. "Christy slammed the door on me again! She is being mean and hurtful and it makes me want to slam the door in her face and let her know how it feels."

There's the sin, big and ugly, and then we can take this to the Lord: "But God I know you've called me to forgive her. And I know work has been stressful for her, and it's hard not to take it out on those at home. I forgive Christy for being mean and slamming the door on me. I give the hurt to you, Lord. I do not want to give this incident to the enemy to use in our lives. Show me if I should mention it to her. I want to forgive her like You forgave me. Help me to walk out this forgiveness and teach me how to love Christy through this."

That's honesty, that's applying the Word of God in truth, and that's healing.

Our daughter's struggle with anger happened many years ago, and she is now free and walks in great joy. In preparation for writing this book,

I asked her how she *knew* that I loved her. I had a list in my mind that I expected her to pull from: "you encourage me, you welcome my friends into our home and love on them, you are eager to hang out with me, etc."

She looked right at me and without hesitation answered, "Because you forgive me. Fully. Whether I seem truly sorry or not, you always forgive me and never hold back your love. Even if I've just asked for forgiveness a few minutes ago, you will help me with whatever I need, or do whatever I'm asking. You don't treat me any differently."

I thought I'd done so many other things to show my love, and this is what meant the most to her? Those other things had been natural expressions of my personality. Forgiveness was not. Forgiveness required a desperate pleading and wrestling with the Lord until my heart submitted to the truths of His Word—and it proved to be the most anointed. In my weakness, He is strong.

Confession

One reason to be gracious to our daughters when they sin is this: we want them to be gracious to us when we sin! For although we are generally more mature than our daughters, there are certainly plenty of times that we sin against them. And what a joy and relief comes when we confess our sins, ask our daughters to forgive us, and they smile and throw their arms around us. "Yes, I forgive you!" Aren't those beautiful words to hear?

A life of repenting to our daughters is honest and freeing - for them and for us. It models the truth of Christianity and creates an environment where we can all grow and flourish.

Sometimes, though, a culture of seeking forgiveness turns sour. It develops when the underlying message behind our repentance to our daughters is this: "I've failed again. I'm just going to fail and fail. Don't expect much from me."

This is not true repentance with the evidence of turning from our sins. This is an Eeyore style of parenting that holds no hope for change.

"Well, another year and I'm behind on your school records. Hopefully you'll be able to graduate in spite of me."

"I blew it again with my daughter. These are the things counseling will have to take care of."

"Uh, no. I don't get involved in all that girl stuff. I didn't have any sisters growing up. I'm not good at it, so I just let my wife take care of it."

"My daughter's hanging out at her friend's house again tonight. Poor thing; we're just not fun parents."

"I can't do any better. My parents weren't good role models."

"I'm not a big talker. It's just not my personality."

There is a certain resignation in these statements and a reluctance to change. Not only is this missing out on the whole-hearted life God has called us to, but it also sends a dangerous message to our daughters when they hear us make these types of comments. My parents are just this way; I shouldn't expect them to change.

This is so contrary to the truths of Scripture where we are exhorted to "...throw off everything that hinders and the sin that so easily entangles. And let us run with perseverance the race marked out for us..." (Heb. 12:1, ESV). Let's let our daughters see us throwing off what hinders us, growing in the Lord, and running hard. It's very difficult to raise daughters for the Lord if we are sitting on the sidelines.

Cohesiveness

We've been talking about working through issues of our hearts when our daughters struggle, but it's more than our own hearts that are affected. A daughter in sin affects the structure and culture of the whole family.

As we are learning to forgive our daughters, even daily if necessary, we must also teach our other children to forgive. Although stress like this in the home is very difficult, it is also an excellent opportunity to teach our other children how to forgive, how to pray effectively, how to be kind in the face of adversity, and how to treat others like we want to be treated.

When our other children have seen one of their sisters disobeying God, it can bring up a variety of emotions in them. They can feel scared; they can feel mad; they can feel like giving up on their sibling; they can feel like crying; they can feel like screaming; they can feel like hiding. They can look at their sister in disgust, in anger, or with compassion. Each sibling is different and it can be tempting to ignore these siblings while we focus on rescuing the struggling daughter.

But no! That is not the path to victory. First of all, that's just setting up our other children for failure. They have questions and concerns that need to be processed with the truth of Scripture so these experiences can be stored in their hearts properly with redemptive purposes instead of destructive memories.

Chandra: Mommy, I don't like the way Tammy's been acting. She just comes home from school and goes straight to her room. She didn't even want to see my new nail polish.

Mom: Don't feel bad. She treats me the same way.

Message: My sister is just irritating.

Chandra: Mommy, I don't like the way Tammy's been acting. She just comes home from school and goes straight to her room. She didn't even want to see my new nail polish.

Mom: I'm sorry, Honey. Her actions have been unkind, and I can see why you're hurt. Usually your sister loves to hang out with you. She's got a lot of schoolwork to do, and she is still learning how to get things accomplished while not ignoring other people. Daddy has been talking to her about this and giving her a lot of great practical suggestions. Let's pray and forgive her and then maybe we could help in some way. I know she loves your famous chocolate chip cookies. How about we make her some to take to school tomorrow? You could even write her a note to put with them.

Message: When my sister is upset, I can help.

Another reason that we don't want to ignore our other children is because we would be overlooking *a great resource of power and prayer.* Let's get our children involved! They already see the situation going on. Ask them to join us in prayer. Ask them to look for ways to bless their sister. Ask them to pray for us that we would have wisdom. We can gather as a family and pray for their sister.

We can encourage our children to apply biblical truths to their relationship. To bring their concerns to their sister in a spirit of gentleness (Gal. 6:1). To specifically encourage their sister (Heb. 3:13). To graciously forgive and interact in kindness (Eph. 4:32).

Jennifer: Oh, Miss Grumpy Pants Kelly has finally come out of her room. Do you want to take some time out of your busy schedule to play a game with us?

Message: My sister has no idea how hard my life is.

Jennifer: Kelly, I noticed that you seem irritated whenever I walk by you and you barely look up from the computer when I talk to you. Have I done something to offend you? I'd really like to know because I love you and I don't want to upset you.

Message: My sister doesn't want to make my life harder.

Sometimes openness and love from a sibling can break down barriers. Sometimes having to explain their own actions to a sibling, especially a younger one, can help our daughters see themselves a little more clearly. Sometimes the constant unconditional love of siblings can help soften even the hardest of hearts, especially if their efforts have been bathed in prayer.

The overflow benefit to training up our other children as a power and prayer team is that we are helping to build biblically strong lifetime relationships in our children. Praying your big sister through a difficult time when she is fifteen builds a path that can be easily travelled when she is twenty-two and turns to ask her little sister to pray about whether she should take a job in a new state. Bringing biblical correction to a sister can help her overcome sinful patterns in her life that would have harmed her future family.

Vanessa: I don't think the stuff you've been watching on the computer lately is good.

Meaghan: What are you, my mother?

Vanessa: No, but if you're going to claim to be a Christian, you need to start acting like one.

Message: My sister is judging me.

Vanessa: I noticed you've been watching a lot of trash on the computer lately. I think you ought to stop.

Meaghan: What are you, my mother?

Vanessa: No, I was just thinking of Psalm 101:3 that encourages us to not put any worthless thing before our eyes. I think what you're watching may be pulling you down. I know you're tired at night, but if you want to go for a walk together instead, I would love to.

Message: My sister loves me and is concerned.

Depending on the age of the children, a sibling can pray, confront, write notes of encouragement, clean her room, clean her car, buy her a small gift, give her a hug, make her a snack, compliment her, encourage her in her giftings, look for attributes to honor in speech and in writing, defend her, invite her to activities, and listen when she talks.

What Destroys Cohesiveness?

One thing that can destroy cohesiveness is slander. We cannot allow our other children to carelessly talk negatively about their sister. And we certainly can't allow it in ourselves! Though we crave sympathy and want to vent our frustrations to everyone we see, we must first take our thoughts to the Lord and to our spouse. Then we can seek counsel from others, but wisdom and discretion must prevail. The emphasis needs to be on how we can change, how we can help our daughters, not belittling our daughters and putting them in a bad light.

Our daughters need to know that we are going to our pastors or a couple of key people for counsel. But they also need to know we believe that we carry the weight of leading our families and that we will be honest about ourselves and seek to make changes in our parenting where we are wrong. Many times these sessions are most helpful if our daughters are present so our counselors can hear their perspectives too. And it's good for our daughters to see our desire to be humble and do all we can to help them. To hear of us slandering them would be destructive to their hearts and to their relationships with us. Let's guard against that.

Another area that needs cohesiveness is our marriage. Wow, can a struggling daughter put stress on a marriage! We are tired, stretched, frustrated, and often times, not agreeing on how to help our daughter. This lack of unity only worsens the situation for everyone involved.

Third John 1:4 says: "I have no greater joy than this, to hear of my children walking in the truth." And boy, is the opposite true too. There is no greater pain than to see our children not walking in truth. The stress is almost consuming.

The best place to start is by praying together; if that's not possible, pray alone and ask God to bring unity. We can evaluate our parenting efforts. Do they line up with Scripture? If not, let's change them immediately. We want God's blessing, not His resistance. We need to confess our failures to the Lord and each other and work to change. We need to forgive each other and seek the Lord afresh for strength and wisdom in raising our daughters.

Compassion, conviction, commitment, confession, and cohesiveness will work together to build a wonderful team that rejoices in our daughter's victories and reaps the benefits as she comes out of her dark season and discovers a family that loved and carried her through it all. And she can then be part of the "support team" when one of her siblings or parents struggles.

"In This World You Will Have Trouble"
(A quote by Jesus Christ—one that's not often
stitched on a living room pillow)[1]

As we write this, Katie has a terrible headache. She had a headache yesterday. And the day before, and the day before that. In fact, every day for over a year, she has had a headache, often accompanied by nausea. Her life, as a senior in high school, was completely interrupted. No birthday party, no finishing high school, no final SAT, no graduation, no further schooling. We have prayed and fasted and cried out to the Lord over and over. The elders in the church have anointed her with oil and prayed many, many times. She has had over thirty medical appointments and tests, but no one has identified or relieved the source of pain yet.

What do we do as parents? Along with caring for her daily physical needs and trying to bring any relief we can, we care for her soul. Because trials in our daughters' lives can have a huge effect on their souls, one of the best ways we can help them is by actively encouraging and refreshing their souls.

Let's be blunt: During times of suffering our theology is tested.

What we know about God is tested. What we believe about His power and sovereignty is tested. What we believe about His goodness is tested. The very foundation of our relationship with the Lord is often tested during suffering.

When is the best time to learn what Scripture says about suffering? *Before* we are in a season of suffering. When we are in pain, when our minds are confused, when we are under attack, it is very difficult to learn and study.

Will our daughters suffer? Jesus says in Matthew 6:34, "So do not worry about tomorrow; for tomorrow will care for itself. *Each day has enough trouble of its own*" (emphasis added). If we know our daughters will face trouble, we should prepare them for it. But how?

We can share stories from the lives of missionaries. YWAM produces a wonderful collection of missionary biographies that are great read-a-louds and open up lively family discussions. We can host missionaries in our homes for a season or even just for dinner. We can watch inspirational movies where obstacles are overcome. We can share stories from our own lives—successes and failures that we've learned from. We can use smaller incidents in our daughters' lives to prepare them for larger ones to come.

Emma: I can't believe I broke my leg at the playground! I was looking forward to Sarah's ice-skating party all month. Now I can't go!

Dad: I know, Emma. I am so sorry. We've been praying for a quick healing every night and the doctors don't think it should take too long.

Emma: But it won't be better before the party!

Dad: This will cheer you up. I'll go get us some mint chocolate chip ice cream. How about that?

Message: Dad wants to cheer me up.

Emma: I can't believe I broke my leg at the playground! I was looking forward to Sarah's ice-skating party all month. Now I can't go!

Dad: I know, Emma. I am so sorry. We've been praying for a quick healing every night and the doctors don't think it should take too long.

Emma: But it won't be better before the party!

Dad: I really don't know why your leg got broken this week. Sometimes our trials are from the Lord to teach us something. Sometimes they're an attack from the enemy. Sometimes God prevents us from going somewhere we shouldn't. And sometimes our trials are just part of living in a fallen world. This is not heaven and we are going to have difficulties. Whatever God allows in our lives, He will carry us through. How we respond is our responsibility.[2]

Emma: But what could be the point of my broken leg?

Dad: Well, let's see what we know for sure. We know according to Romans 8:28 that God will work this for good. And we see in James 1:2 that we are to rejoice in our trials because of what they can produce in us. Sarah will probably be disappointed not to have you at her party. Let's pray for her and see if there is some way you can use this time to bless her.

Emma: Yeah, I was going to make her a friendship bracelet, but I hadn't had time yet. Maybe I could do that this week while I'm lying around.

Dad: Great idea! And how about I go out and pick up your favorite mint chocolate chip ice cream?

Message: Dad wants to cheer me up and
help me to see God's perspective.

Another way to prepare our daughters is by listening to quality teachings with them. *Living Waters Ministries* has excellent materials for adults and older children, and they've printed great tracts and books for younger children. Their material teaches us how to respond to questions by non-Christians, which often mirror our own questions during trials. We can attend lectures and conferences with our children, knowing that although some of the materials may be a little over their heads, God's Word does not return void (Isa. 55:11).

It is crucial that we help our daughters process their sufferings in a truthful/biblical manner. How a trial is processed or stored in their memories can either strengthen or damage their relationship with the Lord for years to come.

After several months of constant pain, Katie and I (Mary Lou) were driving in the car and discussing her pain, praying, and seeing what our next step should be. "Mom," she said, "I am so discouraged. I feel like the pain will never go away."

Up to this point, I had spent most of the past weeks encouraging her, praying, fasting, taking her to doctors, worshipping with her, and massaging her head and shoulders. But at this moment, I believe the Lord led me to gently challenge her.

"Katie, I believe the Lord is going to heal you. We are praying and many others are carrying you in prayer. But you bring up a good point. What will you do if, for whatever reason, God does not heal you? What if I said to you today, 'Katie, this constant head pain is never going to go away?' How would this affect your relationship with God?"

There was silence in the car. "I guess it wouldn't affect it," she quietly said.

"No, Honey. Don't answer so quickly. Think about it. Pray about it. Remember Shadrach, Meshach, and Abednego? They were going to be thrown into the fire, but their response to the king was amazing. 'We know our God will save us from these fiery flames. *But even if He does not*, we will still not worship your idols.'[3] Can you say the same?"

We drove for a long time without conversation. I prayed fervently in my heart, knowing this was a significant moment in Katie's life. Finally, Katie spoke up. "Yes, I would still serve the Lord. He is Lord of my life, no matter how I feel. I would just look for new ways to show joy and bless others and trust that He would still use me."

Parents, we need to be listening to the Holy Spirit as we help our daughters walk through trials and trust Him to lead us each step of the way. There is not a cookie cutter script that works in each situation; instead it is a humble dependence on a God who loves our daughters greatly and a firm confidence that God will give us what we need as we walk this journey with our daughters.

Strategies for Surviving and Thriving in a Storm

Here are some strategies that can bring nourishment to our souls when we feel trapped and lost in the whirling winds and beating rain of a spiritual hurricane.

PRAY — Always the first and most important thing we can do! "The effectual fervent prayer of a righteous man availeth much" (James 5:16 KJV). This is not referring only to the prayers we offer up as we go about our day. This is referring to *fervent prayer*. Passionate crying out to the Lord on behalf of our daughters. Wrestling with the Lord without regard to time or schedule. An expenditure of energy that would be consistent with what we would display if a murderer was leering at our daughter and trying to rip her out of our arms (Don't be deceived: Satan wants to use these trials to steal, kill, and destroy our daughters—John 10:10).

When one of our daughters was struggling with anger, our fervent prayer took the form of sleepless nights, pacing in the living room while everyone else was asleep, and crying out in all forms of prayer.

During Katie's season of constant pain, our fervent prayer has taken a different form. One of our leaders at church was praying for her and recommended that she spend at least one hour of dedicated prayer time each day as she fights through this storm. This challenge to a girl in great head pain? Seems insurmountable, right?

But we know that times of prayer are *always* fruitful and that the battle is not just for her physical health, but for her spiritual health too. So Rich walked this leg of her journey with her. He got up an hour early each day, encouraged Katie to rise also, and then they went hand in hand to seek the face of God. It was amazing to watch our daughter's spirit strengthen as she was daily bathed in prayer and the support of both her heavenly Father and her earthly father. She has confessed many times that she did not think she could do it without her dad there with her. There are rich benefits when our daughters feel we are walking through the storm with them, instead of just waiting outside the circle of winds and yelling directions at them.

FAST — "Is this not the fast which I choose, to loosen the bonds of wickedness, to undo the bands of the yoke, and to let the oppressed go free and break every yoke?" (Isa. 58:6). Are our daughters bound by wickedness? Oppressed? Under a yoke? Then let's stand on this verse and fast with the godly expectation that they will be set free.

ENCOURAGE — Are our daughters becoming hardened? Hebrews 3:13 gives us wisdom: "But encourage one another day after day, as long as it is still called 'Today,' so that none of you will be hardened by the deceitfulness of sin." We can share verses with our daughters through text, phone messages, notes, cards, and engraved gifts.

LOVE — Seems obvious, right? But the truth we learned about communication, that a message is not truly given until the listener receives it, is true about love too. We may think we are showing love to our daughters, but she may not be receiving it.

The 5 Love Languages by Gary Chapman (and all the titles in the series) can be a precious tool in loving our daughters.[4] We are wiser parents if we understand how our daughters receive love—basically through words of affirmation, quality time, gifts, acts of service, or physical touch. We need to express all forms of love to our daughters, of course, but if we can specialize our efforts, we can be more effective. We are going to pour a lot of our time, money, and energy into loving our daughters; why not learn how to channel it in a way that is most powerful in their individual lives?

OBEY SCRIPTURE — Don't obey our daughters. This can be a delicate balance. We want to be aware of their individual needs and respect them, but we are held to a much higher standard. For example, when one of our daughters was struggling with anger, she didn't want us to thank her for doing her chores. "Don't thank me for doing the dishes. I'm only doing them because you make me." Throughout Scripture, though, we see the command to be thankful. So the next time she brought this up, we explained that we understood her request, but still believed we should express thankfulness and build a culture of gratitude in our home because it is pleasing to the Lord.

Over the years, we have had to remind our daughters that the best way we can love them is by obeying Scripture and training them to do the same. J.C. Ryle writes in *The Duties of Parents*, "Parents, do you wish to see your children happy? Take care, then, that you train them to obey when they are spoken to, to do as they are bid…. Teach them to obey while young, or else they will be fretting against God all their lives long, and wear themselves out with the vain idea of being independent of His control."[5]

Honey, you are a precious gift to me, and I will have to stand before the Lord one day and be held accountable for how I raised you. This is a sobering thought. I know you don't agree with the decision I've made. But you have my parenting manual—the Bible. You can see for yourself what the Lord requires of me. If I make my decisions based on a concern about how you might respond, that's called fear of man, and it will prove to be a snare for me and for you. Although I love

*you greatly, I do not love you more than I love God, and I'm
not going to go against His Word just because you want me to.*

EXPECT OUR DAUGHTERS TO OBEY — Here is another one that
seems obvious but is often lost in our culture. Our daughters are to obey us.
Ephesians 6:1-3: "Children, obey your parents in the Lord, for this is right.
'Honor your father and mother' (which is the first commandment with a
promise), so that it may be well with you, and that you may live long on
the earth."

*I understand that you don't agree with me, and I don't expect
you to agree with every decision I make. And that's all right.
You are eleven years old. You don't have the wisdom or the
grace from God to raise an eleven-year-old girl yet, and that's
okay. Your role is clear in Scripture, and that is to obey me.
Now I did not make this up. This is not some ego trip for me
where I decided I would feel more powerful if you had to obey
me. This is God's design and He follows it with a promise:
"That it many go well with you." I want it to go well with you,
I want you to walk in the blessings of the Lord, and I expect
you to obey me.*

DISCIPLINE OUR DAUGHTERS — Hebrews chapter 12:5-11 gives
a beautiful description of discipline as an act of love: "For those whom
the Lord loves He disciplines...If you are without discipline...you are
illegitimate children...We had earthly fathers to discipline us...it yields the
peaceful fruit of righteousness."

If we want our discipline to be blessed by God, we must follow God's
directions. We must use the discipline He describes in Scripture and apply
it with love, purpose, and faith. It's helpful to pray in our hearts before any
discipline and get our own hearts right with the Lord before we take any
action. We are acting as agents of the Lord, and we want to be wonderful
ambassadors of God's redeeming correction.

DISCERN OUR DAUGHTERS' NEEDS — Without a doubt, all of our discipline needs to be founded on God's inerrant, love-filled, life-bringing, eternal words. God's methods producing God's results.

God teaches us, though, that we need to be discerning to determine what our daughters need at the moment. It will depend on our daughters' individual strengths and struggles, motives and memories, age and awareness. For example, if we adopt a four-year-old girl that has a history of abuse, we may handle crying at bedtime differently than we would with a four-year-old born in our secure home where night does not bring back terrifying memories.

Here's a power verse with great directions for parenting with discernment: "We urge you, brethren, *admonish* the unruly, *encourage* the fainthearted, *help* the weak, be *patient* with everyone" (1 Thess. 5:14, emphasis added). Very specific. Very individual. Very powerful.

DON'T TEACH LIES – Okay, no parent sets out to teach their children lies, but somehow they can sneak in.

"I love you *but* I'm going to have to discipline you." No, no, no. That goes directly against Scripture and implies that discipline is the opposite of love. "I love you *so* I'm going to discipline you."

"No, Abby, you can't do that. It's not fair." Is life fair? What about 1 Thessalonians 5:15? "See that no one repays another with evil for evil, but always seek after that which is good for one another and for all people." Well, that's not fair at all! Throughout Scripture, Christians are exhorted to live in a manner that is not fair: turn the other cheek, pray for your enemies, lend without expecting repayment, forgive.

If God calls us to live a distinctly unfair life, why would we want to hold up the standard of fairness when raising our daughters and trying to motivate them? It's a distortion of the Christian life, and one that may leave our daughters struggling when difficulties arise.

DON'T USE GOD AS YOUR SCAPEGOAT — How often do we say: "No, that's not pleasing to God.... No, we're Christians and we don't do that…No, we can't see that, do that, wear that, listen to that, go there, or say that…God says no…Scripture says no…No, no, no!"

Is this going to draw our daughters' hearts to God? Is this the God we know from Scripture?

We tend to accent the positive when we describe ourselves: "Look what *I* bought you. Sure you can go. Who wants Daddy to take them out for ice cream? *I* worked all night and got your dress ready for the dance."

Oh, parents, how quick we are to attribute the no's of life to God and the yeses of life to us. It's wrong and it misrepresents us and God. It is God's kindness that draws men to repentance (Rom. 2:4). The Lord is compassionate and gracious, slow to anger and abounding in lovingkindness" (Ps. 103:8).

Instead, we can say, "I was up praying for you last night and felt God telling me to stay up and finish your dress…We've noticed how kind you girls have been lately and we asked God how we can bless you. So how about a trip to the beach?…Yes, you're right. We could own a much nicer home. But we believe the Lord wants us to invest our money in you and equipping you for the things He has called you to do…God tells us to practice hospitality. Let's have a party!"

V FOR VICTORY – A helpful parenting perspective is the V principle. Picture the line making the right side of the V as the path of righteousness that God desires for your daughter. The line making the left side of the V is the other path. Where these two lines meet at the bottom is the beginning of your daughter's life. She starts at the bottom and journeys up on one of these paths.

One method of parenting would be called crisis parenting. Suddenly something causes you to look closely at your daughter's life, and you see her fairly far up on the left line, quite a distance from the righteous path, and you freak: Crisis! The gap is huge, the stakes are big, and the rescue path is long.

But how does a daughter get so far along on the wrong path? It starts with little choices, little unbiblical attitudes, little lies believed. For down at the bottom of the V, the step over to the wrong path is small, almost imperceptible. But a continued life on that path takes her farther and farther away from the life God desires for her.

The lesson to parents: it's much easier to correct our daughter when the changes are subtle and the lies are just starting to take root. When the lies and ideas have gone deep, when sins have been embraced, when lifestyles have been established, it's much harder to break free.

Explaining this to our daughters can be helpful:

Dramatic, obvious sins start with overlooked hidden sins. Left uncorrected and unrepented, these sins grow and grow until devastation occurs. "But each one is tempted when he is carried away and enticed by his own lust. Then when lust has conceived, it gives birth to sin; and when sin is accomplished, it brings forth death." (James 1:14-15)

So, Hannah, this is why we correct you on what may seem to be small issues. Like rolling your eyes at us, taking money off our dresser without asking, speaking harshly to your sister. We love you and we want you to have a victorious life that is blessed by God. We don't want you to get on the wrong path and suffer the consequences. We don't want you to believe lies now that would one day lead you to destroy your life and the lives of those you love. We want to help you now.

DON'T BE A HYPOCRITE — Every Christian has a ministry, a way that he interacts at some level with the world around him. Whatever our level of ministry, whether it be international or focused only within our small community, this is true: We need to make sure our ministry is validated at home.

During seasons where one of our daughters is struggling and needing extra guidance, we may need to say no to other exciting opportunities. We can structure our family life so that our children get our best, not our leftovers. We want our children to have the comfort of knowing who we are, in the home and outside the home, and knowing that we are honest and genuine wherever we are.

SECURE SUCCESSES — Sometimes if our daughters are having a difficult time in one area, they may feel like a failure in all of life. This is where we as parents can strategically set up areas to succeed. For example, if our daughters are struggling in school, we can give them other arenas to excel in. "Sure, you can try that recipe! Those look like fun, new ingredients. Great meal, Honey. Everybody loves when you cook." We don't want our daughters to be tempted to feel like losers just because one area of life is difficult for them. Instead we want our daughters to feel confident and discover their God-given talents.

CHECK THE HORMONES — If our daughters have been having a particularly troubling time in the pre-teen to teen years, hormones may be aggravating the situation. Notice the word *aggravating* not *causing*. We are called to obey the Lord no matter what season of life we are in, and we know that God gives us everything we need for life and godliness (2 Peter 1:3). But there are certain factors that can make this much harder.

For example, let's say our daughter struggles with laziness. Now we can do all that we can to correct and encourage her to a life of diligence and self-control. But if she has a raging headache while we are addressing her, it's going to be very difficult for our words to break through, and the raging headache is probably magnifying the laziness issue. If we can help alleviate some of her pain, though, then we can be more effective at helping her battle laziness. Hormone imbalance can bring on headaches, significant mood swings, fuzzy thinking, and increased sexual temptations. It may be something to have your doctor check.

DON'T BE OVERCOME — Romans 12:21 says, "Do not be overcome by evil, but overcome evil with good." How does this command affect our responses when our daughters are acting mean? The way our daughters treat us cannot determine how we treat them. That is us being overcome by evil. Instead, we must rise up in kindness and trust that our kindness will help them overcome their struggles.

LET OUR DAUGHTERS SEE US CRYING OUT TO GOD — Our daughters need to see us praying when we are sad, confused, angry, and hurt. They need to know that He is our "go-to guy" when we are struggling. A Christian friend of ours raised two children. Both are grown and she says that neither is living for the Lord. I asked her if, looking back, there was anything she wishes she would've done differently. Her reply was instant: "I didn't teach my children to rely on God. I was an organized and competent mother. They never saw me crying out to God for help, so they never thought they needed God either."

OFFER A SACRIFICE OF PRAISE — What does the Lord want from us when we are in pain and affliction? What will please the Lord during these seasons? "But I am afflicted and in pain; may Your salvation, O God, set me securely on high. I will praise the name of God with song and magnify Him with thanksgiving. *And it will please the Lord* better than an ox or a young bull with horns and hoofs" (Ps. 69:29-31, emphasis added). Worshiping right in the middle of the hard times, when we are exhausted and weary, can bring an amazing refreshment to our spirits as we re-acknowledge that God is God, no matter what our circumstances. We can then let His love flow over us and revive our hearts.

Dear Parents,

Are you tired and weary? Are you confused, disappointed, and exhausted? Are you losing hope and wondering when this will end? Do you feel alone and dejected? Do you feel angry and embarrassed? Do you feel lost and afraid?

I will lift up my eyes to the mountains; from where shall my help come? My help comes from the Lord, who made heaven and earth. Psalm 121:1-2

Does your soul need to be restored? Do you need wisdom? Does your heart need rejoicing? Do you need enlightening? Look to the Word of God:

The law of the Lord is perfect, restoring the soul;
The testimony of the Lord is sure, making wise the simple.
The precepts of the Lord are right, rejoicing the heart:
The commandment of the Lord is pure,
enlightening the eyes. Psalm 19:7-8

Is your home a battlefield?

He who dwells in the shelter of the Most High will abide in the
shadow of the Almighty. I will say to the Lord, "My refuge and
my fortress, my God in whom I trust!" Psalm 91:1-2

Do you feel like giving up?

Do you not know? Have you not heard?
The Everlasting God, the LORD, the Creator of the ends of the earth
Does not become weary or tired.
His understanding is inscrutable.
He gives strength to the weary,
And to him who lacks might He increases power.
Though youths grow weary and tired,
And vigorous young men stumble badly,
Yet those who wait for the LORD
Will gain new strength;
They will mount up with wings like eagles,
They will run and not get tired,
They will walk and not become weary. Isaiah 40:28-31

Have you lost hope?

My soul, wait in silence for God only, for my hope is from Him.
He only is my rock and my salvation, my stronghold; I shall not be shaken.
On God my salvation and my glory rest; the rock of my strength, my
refuge is in God. Trust in Him at all times, O people; pour out your
heart before Him; God is a refuge for us. Psalm 62:5-8

Faith for you and your children:

Praise the Lord!
How blessed is the man who fears the Lord,
who greatly delights in His commandments.
His descendants will be mighty on earth;
the generation of the upright will be blessed. Psalm 112:1-2

Prayer

Heavenly Father, help me to lead my daughter well during seasons of difficulty and pain. May Your grace and truth flow through me when I am helping her to overcome sin in her life, and may I be faithful to repent and seek reconciliation as needed for the sin in my own life. May I be a continual source of encouragement and hope to her when she is in pain or going through trials.

---

[1] From John 16:33 (NIV).
[2] The book of Job is so helpful here.
[3] From Daniel 3:17-18.
[4] Gary Chapman and Ross Campbell, *The 5 Love Languages of Children* (Chicago: Northfield Publishing, 2012).
[5] J.C. Ryle, *The Duties of Parents* (Conrad, MT: Triangle Press, 1996) 20.

The Daughters Speak

Katie Says...

For over a year I've been walking through pain. And I don't know where I'd be if it weren't for the Lord and my family.

Lots of people go through horrible pain that is seriously dangerous. Thankfully, I don't have to be hospitalized or on constant medication. I can't even imagine how hard that would be.

But this journey has been difficult for me. I've had a constant headache and occasional nausea for a long time now. I wasn't able to graduate when I wanted to or get my license when I wanted to. I guess the Lord had different plans for me.

When I have a raging headache, it's hard for me to think clearly. I am very grateful for my parents who speak truth to me while I feel like I am in a fuzzy maze.

One of my foggiest weeks was when I took some prescription drugs the doctor prescribed. I had never taken medication before. The drugs instantly changed my bright and friendly personality into a downcast and solitary personality.

During that week, two of my close friends came by to visit and pray for me. Normally I would run into their arms, ecstatic to see them. Well, not that day. I sat in my parents' room, crying, not wanting to go out and see them. I clearly remember my mom looking me right in the eyes and emphatically saying, "Katie, these are your friends. They love you and you love them. You need to go out and see them. You will regret it later if you don't." I am so glad I went out to see them. But even more than that, I am thankful that my mom was there to speak truth to me.

As was mentioned in this chapter, my dad was a huge help to me when one of the leaders in our church wanted me to pray for an hour every day. I don't think I could've done it without him guiding me and holding my hand.

Another way my dad has helped me and loved me through this season is his honesty and humility. Here are two examples and how they tie together:

My dad would always try to encourage me to try and limit unnatural forms of pain relief and be cautious about getting addicted to anything.

"Aw Katie, you had to take medicine? Ugh, you had to get a Coke for the nausea?"

He would say this with a smile on his face, but I knew he would prefer me take more natural products.

Also, he would encourage me in 1 Thessalonians 5:16-18: " Rejoice always; pray without ceasing; in everything give thanks; for this is God's will for you in Christ Jesus." He would give me pep talks and coach me in this verse.

"What can you learn from this? What do you need to grow in? Katie, we are to rejoice always and give thanks in everything." He would share what he wanted to grow in and try to help me think of ways that I could grow.

Well, a couple months ago my dad got sick and had a headache. He had a headache for two days. Somehow, all those encouraging words and pep talks he had given me hadn't quite stuck in his heart now that he was the one in pain. (Note: when my dad read this part, he quickly drew a smile and scribbled on the manuscript: Don't minimize my suffering!)

When my mom and I would walk into the room, my dad would start moaning and holding his head. Yes! Literally moaning out loud. My mom and I just smiled at each other and helped him in whatever way he needed.

Once the day or so of head pain was over, my dad said he was feeling much better and invigorated after taking some medicine. I mentioned, with a smile on my face, "Well, you know, Daddy, you encourage *me* to rejoice *always* and give thanks in *everything*—even while I'm in pain."

Oooooh…it was as if I suddenly handed him eyeglasses to see himself clearly.

My dad, now knowing how painful a headache can be, eagerly proclaimed, "Katie, if you ever want a Coke, I would be glad to go get you an XL Big Gulp of Coke."

I love how my dad was humble and honest. He was sympathetic before, but now is even more sympathetic to the pain I have.

In conclusion, I'm appreciative that my parents do a great job at comforting me, serving me, giving me massages for hours, doing anything they can think of to help alleviate and rid the pain. But they don't leave me there. They help push me past the pain, help me get stronger, and help me to "Rejoice always; pray without ceasing; in everything give thanks; for this is God's will for you in Christ Jesus" (1 Thess. 5:16-18).

6

Here Come the Girls

Developing Fruitful Friendships

If you have a daughter you know this: having one daughter is like having five. For wherever a girl goes, she is sure to bring another, and another, and another...

Think of couples on a double date. One lady gets up to go to the bathroom. What does she do? She turns to the other lady at the table: "I need to go to the restroom. Do you want to go with me?" The other lady will leap up and they will head off, chatting and laughing all the way to that secret hangout—the ladies' room.

This habit starts early in life; a girl seems to be born with a desire to be around other girls. There are sleepovers, dance parties, cooking nights, study groups, play dates, craft days, birthday parties, skating parties, church parties. There's endless hanging out, endless talking on the phone, and endless movie nights. There's giggling, squealing, crying, and screeching. There are hugs, tears, dancing, and jumping. There are passionate pledges of loyalty, broken promises, and misunderstandings. There's compassion, there's sympathy, there's encouragement. There's life, there's laughter, and there's love, all bubbling, exciting, and overflowing.

There are girls...everywhere you look.

Our home is generally filled with girls. From Mary Lou's eighty-four-year-old mother who lives with us, down to the two-year-old girl we babysit twice a week, to everyone in between. We've had girls over for game nights, girls help us work around the house, and girls pray with us. We've had girls join us for dinner, spend the night, spend the week, spend the month, spend several months. We've been blessed by girls, inspired by girls, challenged by girls, and had great fun with girls.

Our goal has been this: *we want to love our daughters so much that it naturally overflows into love for their friends.* That love can be expressed by an open door, an open heart, and an encouraging word. Let's look together at ways to help our daughters develop fruitful relationships, and let's look at some ways we can develop fruitful relationships with our daughters' friends.

Choosing Wise Friends

"I think you are letting Stephen get away with too much. I know he's your youngest, but he's really not obeying you well." We looked at the fourteen-year-old girl standing in front of us, sharing this blunt analysis, and our hearts felt one thing: thankfulness.

Sarah had spent many years hanging out in our home. Now we had asked for her observations after babysitting our son, and her answer was like gold. We knew she was for us, we knew she respected the rules in our home, and we knew she was right—we were not being faithful to train our son to obey us. It was a well-needed wake-up call, and we thanked her sincerely.

Years later, we got a phone call from Sarah on our drive home from a Bible study. "I'm thinking of going to Alaska to work for the summer. What do you think?" she asked. We had developed, through years of interacting and sharing life together, a mutual respect and friendship that serves us to this day. We value her input and she values ours. How did we get there?

The first step is the friends our daughters choose. Sarah's mom had been praying that God would provide a good friend for Sarah. In fourth grade that friend came, and it was our daughter, Brittany. From our first interaction with Sarah, we saw a strength and sincerity that we knew would make for a loyal friend, so we fostered that relationship.

And that can be one way that we help our daughters. We can draw attention to godly qualities in others and extend the extra time and effort to strengthen these friendships.

Mom: How was your Sunday School class this morning?

Lana: It was hard. Everyone had a box of crayons except for me. But this new girl, Amber, shared her crayons with me.

Mom: That was really sweet of her. Did you ask her for crayons?

Lana: No, she just saw that I was sitting there and not coloring, so she asked if I wanted to share her crayons.

Mom: That is great. What a kind girl. Maybe you can introduce her to me next week, and I'll talk to her mom and see if they could come over some time.

Too often the temptation is to let our daughters develop friendships based on convenience. Just because a girl sits next to our daughter in class or lives down the road does not mean she will be a good friend. Yes, it's easy to say, "Sure you can go home from class with her" or "Go outside and play with the neighbors."

Easy? Yes.

Wise? Not always.

Our daughters' friends will have a huge influence on their lives. Let's look at some of the warnings in Scripture:

Do not associate with a man given to anger;

Or go with a hot-tempered man
Or you will learn his ways
And find a snare for yourself.
Proverbs 22:24-25

A perverse man spreads strife,
And a slanderer separates intimate friends.
Proverbs 16:28

A violent man entices his neighbor
and leads him down a path that is not good.
Proverbs 16:29 (NIV)

Do not be deceived:
"Bad company corrupts good morals."
1 Corinthians 15:33

Scripture clearly tells us to *not be deceived* about the power of bad friendships. But how do we help our daughters choose good friends?

First, in the daily activities of life, we can be teaching our daughters about godly character. We can draw attention to the kindnesses of other girls, do a study together on friendship, share stories from our own childhood about good friends and not so good friends, and discuss the qualities of friendships displayed in books and movies. We want to help our daughters recognize true friendship and deceitful friendships and grow into discerning these differences on their own.

Like in other areas, it is easier to teach our daughters to evaluate friendships if we are involved in their lives. We can get to know other girls, ask them questions, look at their social media pages, get to know their parents, and observe our daughters' interactions with them. This will give us more opportunities to pass on observations infused with the wisdom that we have gained through years of experience and walking with the Lord.

Mom: *How are things going with Aishia? She hasn't been over in a while.*

Kayla: *Things are fine. She's probably just been busy.*

Message: *Mom wanted to know where Aishia was.*

Mom: *I really enjoyed being at your school today.*

Kayla: *Yeah, all the kids loved hearing about your time in Australia.*

Mom: *I noticed you didn't hang out with Aishia at all during the break.*

Kayla: *We never hang out at school. She explained it to me.
We are just neighborhood best friends, not school best friends.*

Mom: *That's interesting...Do you do that with any of your other friends?
Tell them they are only your friend in certain places?*

Kayla: *No, of course not. But Aishia has so many friends
that she has to put them in categories.*

Mom: *Well, Kayla, if someone is truly your friend, then she is your friend
no matter where you are. Why don't you help me make these brownies?
I thought we could take them down to the family that moved in down the
street. I heard they have a daughter your age.*

Message: *Mom cares about my friendships.*

What qualities should we teach our daughters to look for in a friend? Let's look again at Scripture:

A friend loves at all times,
And a brother is born for adversity.
Proverbs 17:17

Faithful are the wounds of a friend,
But deceitful are the kisses of an enemy.
Proverbs 27:6

Finding Godly Friends

This all sounds good, but where are the godly friends? They seem so hard to find.

The answer is easy, but countercultural: broaden the net! Our society has a narrow definition of friends for children: "someone of the same age with the same interests." These walls arose from the time that children spend at school, learning and playing with only children of their own age, and gravitating to children with similar interests during playtime and lunch. This goes on for twelve years until, suddenly—whoosh—they're in the real world where they work, study, and play with people of all ages and backgrounds. This integrated environment is the better model of maturing relationships, and this is the model where fruitful friendships can blossom. Why not teach them to appreciate friends of all ages while they are still young?

Sisters

Our daughters do not need to only have friends that are their own age. If they have sisters, they have a rich deposit of friendships. First of all, sisters can be encouraged to be best friends. Our daughter's sister is to be her friend forever, through every season of life, from childhood to adulthood, from raising chickens in the back yard to raising children of their own. From the mountaintops of the wedding day to the struggles of midlife.

From styling each other's hair to one day embracing the gray, sisters should be there for each other.

Sisters are also to be a testimony to the world as they interact with each other in love. In the book *Making Brothers and Sisters Best Friends*, the Mally children create a biblical vision as they challenge siblings to rise up and pursue God-honoring relationships with each other:

> *This is not just for your sake, not just for their sake, not just for your parents' sake, but for the glory of the Lord, for the defeat of the enemy, and for a dynamic testimony to the lives of everyone with whom you come in contact! Godly families are few and far between in this 'crooked and perverse generation' (Phil. 2:15) in which brothers and sisters are looked upon as irritations, unsolvable problems, and blemishes in your life.*[1]

Sisters' Friends

Sisters can also share their friends. If they've been raised in a home where sharing and hanging out together is cultivated, then sharing friends will be natural.

In our family, there is an open door policy. Not that we never close our doors, but we try to welcome others when they want to come and join us, whatever we are doing. Our oldest, Brittany, was excellent at this and set a tone for the rest of her siblings to follow. When she had friends over, she included her friends in what she normally did, which was play with her sisters. Brittany and her friends would ask the little sisters to play dress up, dolls, or games with them. When a toddler got up from naptime, the older girls would change what they were doing and find a way to include the little one. They created plays together, played cards together, and cooked together.

As the girls got older, something beautiful happened. Though games and laughter still abounded, conversations would turn to issues of the heart, and prayers would be offered up to the Lord together. As parents, we had been involved in a lot of the play times, and more and more the girls would draw us in to talk with their friends about different struggles. Older friends began going on walks with our younger daughters and giving precious and wise counsel. Older friends would invite the younger girls to join them at movies and parties. They would exchange notes and gifts. Younger girls would pray for the older ones and help them choose outfits for the evening's activities.

Our own friendships grew with our daughters' friends as we discussed Scripture and the joys and challenges of living lives pleasing to the Lord. In essence, love blossomed because the various ages and personalities created a beautiful garden where friendships could grow in the soil of mutual encouragement and shared memories, sprinkled with lots of laughter and fellowship.

Loving Our Daughter's Friends

As parents, we try to cultivate this garden by being involved, being supportive, offering wise counsel, and investing our time and money into an atmosphere where this type of love can grow. And we have to say this: our family has been richly blessed by the amazing, godly girls who have become a part of our home and family over the years. We recognize that their examples, respect for us, and love for all our daughters have made our parenting much easier and more fruitful.

This atmosphere doesn't have to be only developed in your home. Maybe you have a daughter on a soccer team. See if you can serve as a coach or assistant. Maybe you can drive the girls out for ice cream after practice. Or maybe you can arrange a beach trip to build team camaraderie. The point is: we need to know the girls our daughters hang out with and look for opportunities to help our daughters and their friends grow in the Lord

Bookshelf Friends

What if you have only one daughter or you don't know many girls? Where can your daughter find godly friends? Well, our daughters have benefitted greatly by many wise girls that are always available; they sit right on our bookshelves!

We have spent our time and money investing in delightful and challenging books to inspire and equip our daughters in ways that we cannot. From *The Secret Keeper*[2] by Dannah Gresh, which lays a biblical foundation for modesty, to *Before You Meet Prince Charming*[3] by Sarah Mally, that helps strengthen a girl's heart during the season of singlehood, to the YWAM biography *Gladys Aylward: The Adventure of a Lifetime*[4], which sets the example of a woman who sacrificed her life for others. These ladies have served our daughters and invested into their lives and we are very thankful.

Adult Friends

Another option is to encourage our daughters to have friendships with other adult ladies. Again, let's not be limited by the age restrictions of a formal school setting. Older women can share their talents and passions with our daughters: antique shopping, crocheting, marathon running, web design. And as they hang out together, these more mature women can talk with our daughters, hear what's going on in their hearts, and encourage them in the Lord.

This type of relationship usually works best if the woman is a trusted friend of Mom, or a trusted leader in your church fellowship who respects parents' authority. Because no matter how "cool" the older woman is, or how much a girl may enjoy hanging out with her, a girl at home is under her parents' authority, and every girl is called by God to honor her parents so that it may go well with her (Deut. 5:16). The *wise* older woman will give biblical counsel and encourage our daughters to love and honor their parents.

We have a wonderful church leader and his wife, Sean and Kim, who have gone out of their way to reach out to Katie. So when Sean needed to go out of town for the weekend, it was natural for Kim to ask Katie to stay with her and help out with her children. We had seen many examples of godliness in Kim and knew it would be great for Katie to serve. We encouraged Katie to be open with Kim and look for opportunities to learn from her.

Katie had a great weekend, and afterwards, I (Mary Lou) called Kim to get her observations. Did Katie serve with a cheerful heart? Was she responsible? Would you want Katie to help you again? How were your conversations with Katie? What topics did the Lord bring up? Was there anything that you saw in Katie that you would want to know about if she were your daughter? Anything at all that gave you concern?

I also talked to Katie and listened intently to her description of her conversations with Kim. Truthfully, I wanted to hear what Kim's counsel was and discuss it with Katie in light of Scripture.

Great and lasting fruit came from Katie's weekend with Kim. One of the insightful questions Kim asked her was what music she listened to during the day. When Kim discovered that Katie listened to Christian music all day, but none of it was worship music, Kim shared with her how important worship music was to her own heart, and challenged Katie to begin worshipping to at least one song a day and see what God does.

Katie applied the counsel and it changed her life. One song quickly turned into two, then three, until now worshipping throughout the day is a way of life for her. All from the suggestion of one wise, older woman.

When we are the mom that other girls are coming to for counsel, we need to remember this: don't say anything to the girl that we wouldn't say in front of her mom. Let there be an understanding that we want to help the girl grow in the Lord, that we respect her parents' authority. We can encourage the girls to talk to their parents, and with younger girls, we may even need to let the parents know what we discovered in our conversations. Remember, the girls' parents are accountable to God for their daughter, so the more they know, the better they can pray and serve their daughter. We can't let our friendships with young girls be an ego boost; we must love them and do all we can to serve them.

When dads interact with their daughters' friends, it is wise to keep this verse in mind: "Abstain from all appearance of evil" (1 Thess. 5:22, KJV). Here are two guidelines that have helped me (Rich): If I need to pick up my daughter's friend, I have someone else ride with us too. And whenever I have a conversation with my daughter's friends, I tell my wife about it and encourage her to follow up with the young girl. I want all our daughters' friends to see my wife and me as one unit.

How Can We Help?

So, what do we do when our daughters find loving and faithful friends? We do all we can to enhance these relationships. Oftentimes, this requires throwing convenience out the window and literally driving that extra mile for the relationships. We can pick up friends and bring them over, invite their whole family over, meet at a park, meet at a mall. We can invite these friends to join in on our family activities and trips. We can invite them to church, to youth group, to girls' Bible studies. Generally it will take effort and sometimes expense from us, but, as we see in Scripture, the cost is well worth it. Don't we want our precious girls surrounded by strong, godly friends that will respect us and love our daughters?

Teach Our Daughters to Be Good Friends

As we are training our daughters to recognize a good friend, we need to be teaching them something else....how to *be* a good friend.

One year, Katie made a new friend at a class she attended. As Katie shared with us their conversations, and as she showed us their email exchanges, we began to grow concerned that their friendship was built on insulting each other. Though we appreciate joking and laughter, a friendship based on mocking and insults would not be profitable. We talked to Katie and examined the emails together to give her examples of our concerns. We felt that this girl was not being a good influence on Katie. We encouraged Katie to limit her interactions and intentionally change the tone of her conversation to one of kindness and encouragement.

As Katie made these changes, an interesting thing occurred. The girl shared that she noticed these changes and that she actually had not enjoyed her relationship with Katie because Katie was so mocking. Although Katie felt the other girl had been the one to set a mocking tone to their relationship, the girl actually saw Katie as the mocker. Katie learned from this incident and has become a young woman that intentionally brings encouragement to everyone she meets.

Just because our daughters find godly friends doesn't necessary mean they will develop godly friendships with them. Our daughters may need to be taught how to talk about the Lord, how to share what's on their hearts, how to share what God is doing in their lives. A girl may have a beautiful, dependable car, but she still has to learn how to drive it. So it is with friendships.

One of the best ways to teach our daughters how to have biblical fellowship is by modeling it for them. As we take an interest in our daughters, ask questions to draw out their hearts and pray for them, they will be *learning through receiving.*

Mom: What did you get from the message this morning at church?

Serena: Pastor Scott did a great job talking about the ways we need to be on guard for pride in our life.

Mom: Yeah, I thought his list was great too.
Why do we need to watch out for pride?

Serena: Because God opposes it.

Mom: Right! Who wants to be opposed by God?

Serena: Not me!

Mom: So, from the list Pastor gave us, in what area do you think you are most tempted to be prideful?

Serena: Well, I'm guessing with my brothers.
They do such dumb stuff and it drives me crazy.

Mom: How could that be pride?
It's true that your brothers can be loud and messy.

Serena: Yeah, well Pastor said if we look down on the actions of others,
that's pride. So I guess that's what I do.

Mom: I think you're right. The fact that you said your brothers do "dumb
stuff" is an indication that you are looking down on them and judging
their actions. You are assuming the girly things you do are just fine, but
the things they do are wrong. Yes, that's pride. You need to give your
brothers room to be boys and explore their God-given desires to explore,
conquer, and protect, just like you want to have room to cultivate your
feminine interests and express your creativity all over the house.

As conversations like these become common in our homes, our daughters will naturally learn skills to help examine their own hearts and have heart-to-heart talks with their friends.

When your daughters are trying to take a friendship to a deeper level, honesty and humility can open up many hearts. Questions like these can build biblical fellowship between friends:

- So, what have you been reading in Scripture lately?
- My sister pointed out to me that my laziness in keeping my side of the room clean is really bothering her. Every time I've come over to your house, your room is always so neat. How do you keep it that way?
- I am feeling really overwhelmed in school, and I don't think I can keep up with my schoolwork and chores at home. Would you pray for me?
- I felt God wanted me to pray for you tonight. Is there something specific I can pray for?
- I was praying for you last night, and this verse came to my mind.

Can I share it with you?

- I've felt really challenged lately that I am living a spoiled life and have become blind to the needs of others. My church is doing a homeless outreach this weekend, and I'm going to join them. Would you like to come with me?
- I just got this great new book, and I was wondering if you'd like to read it too, and we could discuss it each week.

Book Studies

Book studies are a wonderful way to springboard conversations and learn from each other. When Brittany was about twelve, I (Mary Lou) found a resource from Doorposts called *Beauty and the Pig*, which is based on understanding true beauty as described in Proverbs 11:22: "As a ring of gold in a swine's snout so is a beautiful woman who lacks discretion."[5] This study book is written to young girls and directs them to read and answer questions based on Scripture.

I thought it would fun to include others, so I invited one of Brittany's friends and her mom to join us. We kicked it off with a trip to the mall to get free makeovers and learn to subtly enhance our God-given beauty. Then we met regularly at a café to discuss the book and our insights from the Lord.

This was a precious time of our daughters sharing their struggles and insecurities, us moms sharing our own struggles and insecurities, and a knitting of our hearts as we encouraged each other and prayed for each other throughout the week. It was a great training ground for Brittany as she and I were able to discuss our meetings on the drive home. I watched with joy as she began stepping up and offering biblical counsel and learned to receive input from others.

Sometimes we are in seasons of life where inviting others to join us is not practical. That's fine too. Katie and I did this same study with just the two of us, and we followed our study each week with a special sweet treat or a shopping trip. God delights in blessing us, and so we want to extend that generous spirit to our daughters too, especially as they are pursuing the Lord.

Another great book to study is *Lies Women Believe and the Truth That Sets Them Free* by Nancy Leigh DeMoss.[6] This is one of my favorite books ever. I led a large adult study through this, and I led a group of Becky's young adult friends on a journey through this book. The girls, all singles, ranged in age from nineteen to twenty-five. Rich took our younger children out to play tennis, and I made dinner ahead of time. When the girls arrived each week, we met in the living room and opened with prayer and a sharing of what God had done that week in our lives. Then we discussed that week's chapter and the questions that I had given to them the prior week. When Rich and the younger children got home, we all hung out together and had dinner.

Oh, the insights these girls had! It was beautiful to watch them open up about struggles, encourage each other, and grow in their understanding of the Lord and their love of truth. At the end of each night, I would give each girl an index card to write her name and a specific prayer request about her own heart. Then I would pray, shuffle the cards, and hand out one to everyone. I participated in this too (and I also totally participated in sharing my struggles and the ways the Lord was speaking to me). Then the card we each received would be our prayer emphasis for the week. On the back of the card, we would write what we prayed for the girl and write down a verse or whatever the Lord showed us. Then we would give these back to the girl at the next meeting. I still have my own cards, and the words of encouragement written by these young ladies each week is a precious treasure to me.

What Are We Modeling?

If we find our daughters resistant to input from others, we need to look first at ourselves. Do we have lives that model a hunger to learn more about the Lord? Do we demonstrate lives that seek input from others and value correction and encouragement?

I was sitting in the backyard reading one morning when a couple of my children came running outside. "Quick, Mom, go take a shower! Mrs. Phillips just called. She will be in our area and can meet for lunch." I rushed inside and headed to the bathroom as my children called after me, "Don't worry, we can get our own lunch. Take your time. Everything will be fine here."

Why did my children leap to action and encourage me to head out to lunch with Mrs. Phillips? They don't know her well at all. So why the excitement?

Because my children know this: Mom loves and respects Mrs. Phillips. Mom meets with Mrs. Phillips when Mom is struggling. Mom often cries with gratefulness as she shares about her many talks with Mrs. Phillips and how Mrs. Phillips loved her enough to correct her and help her to fight sin in her life. The children know that Dad is very thankful to Mrs. Phillips for her investment in his wife. Mom comes home encouraged and stronger in the Lord. It is good for the whole family when Mom meets with Mrs. Phillips!

We speak to our daughters every day. Sometimes we use words. But our actions are louder.

Avoiding Familiar Pitfalls

There are many activities that are common for girls, which may not be beneficial to their friendships or their relationships with the Lord. Sleepovers, social media, parties, and dances are good examples. These are considered a "right of passage" to proper girlhood, but are they wise? The answer is different in every case. It can depend on our daughter, the other girls involved, and the specific environment they are in. With so many variables, what's a parent to do?

First of all we need to live in the light ourselves, and train our daughters to do the same. Look at this exhortation from 1 John 1:6-7: "If we say that we have fellowship with Him and yet walk in the darkness, we lie and do not practice the truth; but if we walk in the Light as He Himself is in the Light, we have fellowship with one another, and the blood of Jesus His Son cleanses us from all sin." We need to live in the light; let there be no hidden or dark areas in our lives.

As parents we can do this by openly sharing our struggles and victories with our spouses, and where appropriate, with our children. We can make sure our spouses have passwords to all of our technological access points. We can copy our spouse on emails to the opposite sex. We can declare to our spouse that he or she has the right to ask us about any area of our life without any negative repercussions from us. For the heart of the matter is this: If we are trying to keep something hidden, it's usually for evil intent and our enemy will jump on it.

We can teach and model this principle for our daughters, and require them to embrace it until they become mature enough on their own to seek light in all areas of their lives. For example, when social media burst on the scene, our parenting had to change. The influences on our daughters' lives could now come from all directions. We had to intentionally change our parenting, and our lives, to make time to monitor and discuss these mediums.

Do you have passwords to your daughters' accounts? A story comes to mind here that I (Mary Lou) must share. My adult daughters that live at home have all given me their passwords. I have tried to never do anything with my access that could be embarrassing. Note the word *tried*.

One day Becky was in California for several weeks staying with friends, and I wanted to Skype. I had never used Skype before, but I had seen a button for it on Brittany's Facebook. Brittany was at work, so I went into her account, set up Skype, and sent a message, *I thought*, to Becky in California: "Do you want to Skype?" and signed my name.

Well, apparently, I did something wrong. My sweet message to Becky, "Do you want to Skype?" accidently got sent to every one of Brittany's Facebook friends! Within two minutes, I got an email from a married man we know: "Mary Lou, do you really want to Skype with me?" A minute later, a young teenage boy emails me: "Mrs. Graham, did you want to Skype?" The messages just kept coming. I was so embarrassed, and I apologized profusely to Brittany when she got home as my family laughed hysterically.

Having our daughters' passwords is wise. Some will resist this saying "I need my privacy. Don't you trust me? I'm old enough to not need you looking over my shoulder all the time."

Sometimes we have to remind our daughters of what our adult life actually looks like: "Honey, I'm an adult and a father with seven children. Do you think I do whatever I want, whenever I want? Do you think I just have secret Facebook accounts that Mom knows nothing about? Do you think I send texts that I don't want Mom to see? And if I did, would that be wise? Even the company I work for has barriers on my computer; they don't let employees go to any sites they want. Accountability is all around us, and the wise person welcomes this accountability knowing that it's the deeds done in darkness that can be the most dangerous."

Life lived in the light is not for babies; life lived in the light is for all mature followers of Christ. Life lived in the light is not for children as defined by age; life lived in the light is for all children of God. See how this verse, following the passage on walking in the light that we read earlier, captures who this is for, and why: "My little children, I am writing these things to you that you may not sin" (1 John 2:1a). Can you hear the Father's heart? It's not a restrictive hovering based on a desire to suffocate our lives. It's based on an abounding love that wants us to succeed and not fall into the pitfalls of our flesh and the enemy.

Besides living in the light, we need to be wise about the activities our girls participate in. For example, dance lessons can be a "sacred cow" for American girlhood. International speaker, Dani Johnson, addresses this in her book *Grooming the Next Generation for Success*. The chapter entitled "The Wake-Up Call" says this: "If you've been to a dance studio or a dance recital at one time or another, you've seen how little girls are taught to dance…They dress them in alluring costumes and train them to move their bodies in a sexy manner…Parents, we've sat back and applauded at those recitals long enough."[7]

Are all dance lessons and studios damaging? No, of course not. The point is we need to evaluate each environment before we blindly send our daughter in—whether it be a dance studio, Facebook, or a lock-in at church. We need to ask God to help us *see* the importance of wisely choosing where to send our daughters, give us the *strength* to examine the opportunities, give us the *discernment* to make a decision, and give us the *courage* to love our daughters enough to say no when we need to.

So let's enjoy a life filled with girls and be faithful to point every girl in our home to the God who loves her beyond her wildest dreams. May our homes and our lives be living testimonies!

Prayer

Lord, please help us to find godly friends for our daughter and help us to train her to be a godly friend to others. Let us do everything we can to enhance these friendships, even if they are inconvenient for us. Help us to avoid any activity that might be common for girls but would hinder our daughter's relationship with You. And may each of us walk in the light in all areas of life.

[1] Sarah Mally, Stephen Mally, and Grace Mally, *Making Brothers and Sisters Best Friends* (Cedar Rapids: Tomorrow's Forefathers, Inc., 2006).

[2] Dannah Gresh, *Secret Keeper* (Chicago: Moody Press, 2002).

[3] Sarah Mally, *Before You Meet Prince Charming* (Cedar Rapids: Tomorrow's Forefathers, Inc., 2006).

[4] Janet Benge and Geoff Benge, *Gladys Aylward: The Adventure of a Lifetime* (Seattle: Youth With A Mission Publishing, 1998).

[5] Pam Forster, *Beauty and the Pig* (Gaston, OR: Doorposts, 2003).

[6] Nancy Leigh DeMoss, *Lies Women Believe and the Truth That Sets Them Free* (Chicago: Moody Press, 2001).

[7] Dani Johnson, *Grooming the Next Generation for Success* (Shippensburg: Destiny Images Publishers, Inc., 2009) 56-57.

The Daughters Speak

Stephanie Says...

I'm the youngest girl in our family and I LOVE it! Ever since I was little, my sisters have done an incredible job including me in whatever they were doing. From playing Barbies and dress-up, to going to the movies and evangelizing. I feel very included and very loved!

Because my sisters include me in so many of the things they do, I have gotten to become friends with their friends as well. This has been a wonderful experience for me because I've gotten to learn from many godly women older and more mature than I.

For example, one friend, Sarah, who is nine years older than me, has been a wonderful blessing. She has taken me on a walk and shared wonderful advice, and when she was away in Alaska, she wrote me a sweet letter that I'll treasure forever. She also included all my sisters and me in her wedding as bridesmaids, with Brittany being the Matron of Honor.

Not only do I hang out with my older sister's friends, but they hang out with my friends too. My friends are Katie's friends. My friends love hearing Becky tell stories, going out evangelizing with her, and playing games. They also love hanging out with Brittany and her whole family. They ask about my sisters, pray for my sisters, and are friends with my sisters.

My parents are very involved with our friends as well. They are second-parents to so many girls. Some call them Mom and Dad or "MamaG" and "PapaG" as they have affectionately become known. So many see Mom and Dad as godly role models that they aspire to be like when they have families of their own.

All our friends love talking with my mom. We encourage them to share their struggles with her because we know that God has blessed Mom with much wisdom, and she is a great person to encourage these young women in the Lord. There are a lot of girls with broken families and broken hearts. I'm so glad that God allows my parents to be instrumental in healing their hurts.

My parents don't just speak into their lives; they have fun with them too. When we watch late night movies with our friends, Mom and Dad will often join us. They invite our friends on beach trips and love to play games with us and our friends. They are very hospitable in sharing their house, food, and time with these many girls.

Recently a thirty-three-year-old Japanese missionary came to stay with us for three weeks. When she left, we all cried, thinking about what a great time we had with her and how we would miss her. Before she came, a new Christian from North Carolina stayed with us for a week, and before her, a longtime girlfriend from Haiti stayed with us for several months.

I love getting to be around all these young women who want to live for God, and I know that God will use these friendships to help shape and develop me for the life He's called me to. I am blessed to have all of these friends speaking into my life and encouraging me in my walk with God. I am so grateful to my parents for creating an atmosphere of sharing, hospitality, and love in our home. I am also very blessed to know that my lifelong friends, my sisters, love me very much and will always be there for me.

7

Here Come the Boys

Learning How to Truly Love

"I'm interested in your daughter." Daniel looked up at us briefly, then looked down and continued twisting his hat.

The evening had begun with his simple request: "I'd like to talk to both of you privately." We were not surprised. Daniel was a close family friend and had sought counsel from us many times.

As we sat down, he began talking about his plans and what he felt the Lord was leading him to do. Then Daniel revealed his true desire: "When praying and talking about my future, I feel I must be completely honest. I'm interested in your daughter."

Rich and I stole a quick glance at each other. Words flew back and forth between us on an invisible highway—a communication network laid on the foundational mystery of "two becoming one." Over twenty years of marriage, over twenty years of working through issues when we didn't feel like it, praying when we wanted to run, crying and clinging to the Lord in times of turmoil, and marveling together at the fruit along the way. These had built a path that transcended time and location. In that one look, we poured out our hearts, but Daniel heard not a word.

Brittany will be so excited! Remember a couple of months ago when she was crying and telling us how she felt about Daniel?

We've been praying for them so much.

Remember her prayer? "If he's not to be my husband, please take away this desire."

Daniel is so talented and passionate for the Lord. Brittany seems perfectly gifted to serve with him.

This is all nice, but we are talking about our little girl!

Is she ready?

I don't know. Are we ready?

Rollercoaster

The answer was "no." We were not ready. It was an emotional rollercoaster. We were surprised by the challenges that arose during Daniel and Brittany's relationship, but as we've talked to other parents we learned that courtship and wedding planning are often stressful and emotionally explosive. In most families, conflicts and unmet expectations arise and hearts are hurt.

But how could this be? Two strong Christians that love the Lord... perfect, right? Well, it's also two sinners entering into a new relationship and bringing their own personal histories and expectations, their own strengths and weaknesses. Add to that two families being thrust into a relationship where natural loyalties and preferences reign...oh, it can be a mess!

And don't forget the enemy. Does he want two followers of Christ to begin dating, walk in purity, and bring honor to the name of the Lord? Does he want them to be joined in holy matrimony and be a living example for the whole world to see of Christ's love for the Church as described in Ephesians 5:25-33? No, our enemy does not!

There can be battles from within and battles from without. We learned many things along the way. Some we learned from the wonderful examples of others and the teachings of Scripture. Some we learned from obeying the specific promptings of the Holy Spirit. Some we learned by failing miserably.

Dating is a controversial subject; many dedicated Christians disagree on the details. *The purpose of this chapter is not to establish a relationship prescription that all families must follow.* Instead, we want to share some successes and failures and encourage you with a few things we wished we'd known before we stepped on that crazy, scary, wonderful rollercoaster called *My Daughter is Dating!*

Courting...Schmourting

When Brittany and Daniel began their relationship, they called it "courting." This word may conjure up images of Spartan legalism. For others it carries an almost prophetic power assuring God's blessing on any couple that says they're courting, no matter what they do in private. Call it dating, intentional dating, integrity dating, dating with a purpose, or even courting. Whatever the word, it doesn't matter; the Lord looks at the heart, and that's where our focus needs to be too.

I (Mary Lou) read Joshua Harris' book *I Kissed Dating Goodbye* when Brittany was only eleven years old.[1]

Wow, she was a little young to be in a relationship, don't you think?

Well, I was just doing advance research. "And do not be conformed to this world," the Bible says in Romans 12:2, "but be transformed by the renewing of your mind, so that you may prove what the will of God is, that which is good and acceptable and perfect." Rich and I had dating relationships that were careless and destructive. We didn't want that for our daughters. But what else was there?

If we were going to raise God's girl in His way, with His power, for His purposes...we needed help. *We needed to prepare for this upcoming season of life and let God build convictions in us before we were left to mindlessly follow the patterns set by this world.*

So I began reading Joshua's book to learn about "courtship." I learned that successful dating is not about trying to follow a certain set of rules. It's about understanding that God loves us and when He says no, it is because He is calling us to something far better. It's about loving God and trusting Him. It's about treating all people with honor and respect. It's about making choices with confidence and not settling for counterfeits as we follow God's vision for our lives. Desiring an intimate relationship is not wrong; walking in one before marriage is wrong. C.S. Lewis captures our tendency to settle for less than God's best in this great quote:

> *Indeed, if we consider the unblushing promises of reward and the staggering nature of the rewards promised in the Gospels, it would seem that Our Lord finds our desires, not too strong, but too weak. We are half-hearted creatures, fooling about with drink and sex and ambition when infinite joy is offered us, like an ignorant child who wants to go on making mud pies in a slum because he cannot imagine what is meant by the offer of a holiday at the sea. We are far too easily pleased.[2]*

My Daughter Doesn't Have a Biblical Vision for Relationships...and Neither Do I

A compelling, biblical vision is imperative for our daughters to successfully navigate through the rough waters of relationships.

But wait a second. Do you know what can be the biggest hindrance to building a godly vision in our daughters' hearts? Our own lack of vision. A lack of looking at our past relationships through the lens of truth—God's Word.

Many of us have not gone back through our memories and "restored" them biblically. We need to see our past activities through the truth of God's standards and re-input them into our memories accurately. We may be holding on to ungodly events or relationships as "cool," "exciting," or even "romantic." If that's what we're doing, our discussions with our daughters will lack passion and commitment as we present them with God's instructions for relationships. If we are still holding on to times of immorality as "fun," it will be hard to inspire our daughters to take a different path. Remember, our daughters can sense hypocrisy!

So let's be specific. Let's say you remember a night. A night before you were married. A night after a movie, hanging out in the car with your date, physically involved, and very excited. Wow, what a night!

But let's look at it through God's eyes, the eyes of eternal truth. Lust was exploding in the car that night. In Matthew 5:28, Jesus says, "but I say to you that everyone who looks at a woman with lust for her has already committed adultery with her in his heart."

How did God see that evening? He was there too. Did He see it as a night of romantic passion? Or did He grieve for your night of sin?

One of our first steps as parents can be applying biblical truths to our memories, seeking forgiveness where we need to, studying Scripture, and maybe even seeing for the first time God's beautiful design for relationships. That's why reading books on biblical dating can be helpful before you even suggest them to your daughter.

If you think your past still has a hold on you and affects your ability to embrace the truths of God's Word, *Lord, I Want to Be Whole* by Stormie Omartian can bring clarity and hope as the author shares openly about her own life and walks you through the process of praying, repenting, and releasing all memories to God.[3]

Is Virginity Enough?

What is a biblical vision for guy/girl relationships? Is it simply virginity until the wedding day? Or is there something much richer and more beautiful?

"Every relationship for a Christian is an opportunity to love another person like Christ loved us," says Joshua Harris in *I Kissed Dating Goodbye*.[4]

Sometimes as parents, in our eagerness to protect our daughters' purity, we suddenly become the "relationship police" and throw on them all kinds of rules. It is no wonder that our daughters are tempted to rebel.

Instead, Scripture provides magnificent instructions on how we are to treat *all* people. These can be taught to our daughters and encouraged throughout their entire lives—in their interactions with us, friends, siblings, grandparents, teachers, neighbors, store clerks, pastors, church visitors, bosses, and co-workers. Every day opens up an opportunity for our daughters to choose to treat others in a manner that reflects Christ's love. It starts with her years as a toddler when she learns to share her toys and continues through every season of life.

Let's look at some of the examples from Scripture on how we are to treat others:

Be kind,

do nothing from selfishness,

put others' interests ahead of your own,

be compassionate,

walk in the light,

make no provision for the flesh,

do not slander,

do not pay back evil for evil to anyone,

don't put a stumbling block in a brother's way,

don't be jealous,

encourage one another in the Lord,

and pray for one another.[5]

Great rules for all relationships. These are not God's suggestions. These are how God *tells* us to treat others. Now imagine if these rules overflowed to dating relationships. Read each one again in light of guy/ girl relationships. Applying these truths would revolutionize the Christian dating scene. So much hurt and compromise could be avoided. As our daughters apply these verses to *all* relationships, their dating habits will naturally be more pure and biblically healthy.

This is so much more than just desperately clinging to pre-marital virginity. This is embracing a life of *virtue*. Webster's Dictionary of the English Language describes virtue as "moral excellence."[6] Our daughters have a high calling on their lives—to bring glory to God in *every* relationship, including those with young men ("Whether, then, you eat or drink or *whatever you do*, do all to the glory of God" 1 Cor. 10:31, emphasis added).

Yes, Christians have freedom, but look what that freedom is for: "*For you were called to freedom, brethren; only do not turn your freedom into an opportunity for the flesh, but through love serve one another. For the whole*

Law is fulfilled in one word, in the statement: 'You shall love your neighbor as yourself'" (Gal. 5:13-14 italics mine).

Let's begin today, no matter how old our daughters are, to teach them what the Lord says about relationships. Let's explain to our daughters what love is as biblically defined and let's train them to walk in these truths—with all people.

Helping Our Daughters Know God's Love and Walk in His Power

We can teach our daughters the best we can, but they need a personal revelation of God's expansive love for them. We can battle for this in the spiritual realm:

*For this reason I bow my knees before the Father, from whom every family in heaven and on earth derives its name, that He would grant [my daughter], according to the riches of His glory, to be strengthened with power through His Spirit in the inner man, so that Christ may dwell in your hearts through faith; and that you, being rooted and grounded in love, may be able to comprehend with all the saints what is the breadth and length and height and depth, and to know the love of Christ which surpasses knowledge, that you may be filled up to all the fullness of God. (*Ephesians 3:14-19)

If our daughters understand that God loves them and wants the best for them, they will have more strength to fight temptations. We can help them see that God wants marriage to be a union between two people that are committed to each other forever. To create an environment where each person can fully give body and heart joyfully and without restraint. Knowing what God has designed for marriage will make it easier for our daughters to say no to the sin that tempts them before marriage.

My Own Marriage Stinks...How Can I Inspire My Daughter?

Desiring a godly marriage is great. But it is not marriage itself that offers a life of fulfillment; it is a life of obedience to God's Word. Parents, let's be honest. Marriage is not always that "safe haven" of emotional and physical unity that the Lord intended. And sometimes our own experiences can taint our enthusiasm for presenting God's view of holy matrimony.

But a look back at Deuteronomy 6 can re-inspire us. We have a job to do as parents and that is to walk with our children and talk with our children about the Lord, who He is, and what He requires of us. We are to teach our daughters about God and His eternal truths found in Scripture. That is our calling. It can be so tempting to let the failures in our own marriages give us a jaded view on this unity and leave us with lower expectations and enthusiasm for our daughters' marriages. We can be tempted to let our experiences define our "truth" instead of letting the Word of God define it.

Our daughters deserve better than that. They should not have to be weighed down by negative views on marriage caused by our baggage. Yes, it's good for us to share openly about struggles in our marriage, but we need to share our stories laced with redeeming truths.

Sherry: Mom, how was your date last night with Dad?

Mom: Terrible. Your father is at it again.
We just argued all night. He's driving me crazy.

Message: Marriage is miserable.

Sherry: Mom, how was your date last night with Dad?

Mom: Not that good. Dad and I disagreed all night. We are going to meet
with the pastor next week so he can help us get some clarity.

Message: Couples will struggle, but they get help when needed.

What if your marriage really is miserable? Number one, get help—as a couple or by yourself. As long as we have breath, we need to be throwing off the sin that so easily entangles us and running the race that is set before us (Heb. 12:1). Part of that race is choosing to love our spouse and fulfilling our wedding vows.

Second, because we are raising God's girl, we need to be faithful to give her God's view on marriage. Remember, she is a gift from Him and we are raising her for Him according to His Word. Let's not let the sin in our own marriages hinder our children from experiencing all God has for them. Let's hand them a golden baton, washed in the blood and forgiveness of Christ and strong in His truths, not a rotten apple that we toss at them and say "hope it works out better for you than for us." Let's take our own pain and disappointment to the cross and renew our minds regularly so that we may be faithful in helping our daughters have a vision to embrace virtue and have hope and excitement as they look towards their own marriage.

Fathers

Before a daughter has a relationship with a potential husband, she has a relationship with her father, possibly brothers, and male friends. Her understanding of men, and her preparation for marriage, is built through all of these relationships.

As fathers, our role is crucial here. We've already discussed how we are to demonstrate to our daughters the father heart of God. Our actions will also serve as a living demonstration of Christian husbandry. Our life, our choices, our responses, and our priorities are helping to create in our daughters an expectation of what their own husbands will be like. We want our daughters to benefit from living in a home with a leader that loves the Lord, walks in humility, serves willingly, and courageously spreads the gospel. We want her to have that leader now...and when she is married. The truth is a girl that is not cherished by her father and not led with loving leadership is more likely to accept poor treatment from young men and enter into damaging relationships.

Jake is a twenty-four-year-old newlywed. He says this about dating his wife before they were married: "When I saw how protective her father was, it helped me realize how truly valuable she was. It made me want to fight even harder for her." We can live in a way that reminds our daughters, and others, that they are God's girls and they should be treated that way by their father and by their suitors.

One way to help our daughters mature socially is by providing godly, fun environments for them to cultivate friendships with girls and boys. One of the easiest ways to do this is by fellowshipping with other families and creating contexts where people of all ages play and talk together. Birthday parties, picnics, beach trips, book studies, game nights, camping trips—all of these and many more can be excellent opportunities for our daughters to have healthy friendships with boys while we as parents are also involved and giving needed counsel and boundaries.

Sadly, there are many children who have been mistreated or abused in seemingly safe Christian environments. We need to establish boundaries for our daughters and possibly role-play with them how to respond if someone tries to pull them off alone. More and more today, crimes against young girls are perpetrated by adults they know and trust. We can serve our daughters by establishing boundaries that apply, no matter who the other person is. For example, maybe teaching our daughters not to be in a room alone with another boy/man or not to leave a party with someone other than the one with whom they came. We can't protect our daughters from every predator, but we can give them the skill set and confidence to handle themselves wisely. We need to also tell them many, many times that if anyone ever does anything to them that makes them uncomfortable, we need to know about it right away. And teach them that *if someone tells them not to tell their parents, that's their cue to run to us immediately and tell us everything.*

Opening up our home for activities has been a great venue for me (Rich) to support our daughters' interests, and to get to know the young men in their lives. I make these nights a priority and ask the young men what God is doing in their lives and what books they are reading. I find out what interests them and learn about their goals and desires. I play games and compete with them at various activities, anything to have fun and open up conversations.

I'm not sure how hospitality has been relegated to the women's ministry in most churches. The Bible makes it very clear that we are *all* to "be hospitable to one another without complaint" (1 Peter 4:9). Even more specifically, one of the qualifications for any *man* aspiring to the office of overseer is that he is hospitable (1 Tim. 3:1-2). Dads, if we are not good at showing hospitality, the Bible tells us exactly what to do in Romans 12:13—*practice*!

For some of us, it may be challenging to draw out young men in conversation. If this is an area of weakness, Dale Carnegie's book *How to Win Friends & Influence People* can help.[7] Although written over seventy years ago, he explains and builds upon the powerful and biblical principle that we need to take an interest in others and consider them as more important than ourselves if we want to be successful in relationships.

I want all young men to know that I am involved in my daughters' lives. And I want all potential suitors to know that if they want to spend time with my daughters, they'll be spending time with me.

Brothers

Brothers are an excellent resource for preparing our daughters for healthy relationships. Boys, of any age, think differently than girls. It's true as toddlers, and it's true as adults.

Note from Mary Lou: Where women can often go wrong is by assuming our way of thinking is more mature. "Boys will be boys," we say as we shake our heads and roll our eyes. A book that reveals the needs and desires of men is *Wild at Heart* by John Eldridge.[8] I wish I had read this before I was married, because even in my twenties I still did not understand and value the unique characteristics of a man's heart. Both of our older daughters have read this book, and we all agree that we learned more about the hearts of men, and even more about our own hearts.

In marriage, women are called to respect their husbands (Eph. 5:33). Our daughters do not need to respect their brothers in the same way they will respect their husbands, but they can learn to appreciate and value male leadership, strength, and wisdom.

In our family, we've had to be especially creative with this because all our boys are younger than their sisters. The girls are usually in the babysitting role, which can lead to a bunch of girls that are very comfortable bossing around young men. We've had to be intentional in helping the girls honor godly character qualities in their brothers and seek their advice and counsel when appropriate.

I'm teaching a kids' class on Sunday morning about the life of Paul. What do you think I could do to make the class more engaging?

You did great on the field today. That was an awesome catch!

Do you think we should play games or watch a movie while Mom and Dad are out tonight?

I still can't get my serve over the net. Will you help me?

You do such a great job talking to my friends when they come over. They're always telling me what great brothers I have.

Would you pray for me? I have to take a test today.

This perspective on brothers serves two purposes: it helps our daughters cultivate thankfulness and respect, and it helps our sons grow stronger in godly character. It's a win-win!

Consider Hudson Taylor, the missionary credited with starting China Inland Mission and opening up that country to the gospel. A hero of the faith. But he was once a young, unsaved rebel...with a sister. A sister who loved God. And what was she doing? Praying for him three times a day until he was saved.[9]

The Botkins crystallize the importance of the brother/sister relationship in their book *It's (Not That) Complicated*: "Today every corner of the globe is crying out for great men. Those of us who have brothers need to recognize the incredible opportunity and responsibility we have been given – to invest in the lives of tomorrow's greatest men. It might be one of the most important things you will ever do."[10]

We've Talked About Our Daughter, but What About Us?

Since we are talking parent-to-parent here, let's talk about an often-overlooked subject: the effect on us when our daughter is in a dating relationship.

The first struggle is fairly obvious: our daughter is entering a new season of life and she's taking us along with her—maybe dragging us along with her! Although we can look forward to this season, it may still seem to come upon us suddenly. There is another adult in the mix now, and his opinions and convictions must be considered. We must share our daughter with another man.

It is tempting to be so self-focused and sad that our little girl is growing up that we don't release her to enjoy herself. We must guard against making our daughter feel guilty for going out, spending time with his friends and family, and investing the time necessary to cultivate new relationships. We can serve our daughter best if we position ourselves to enthusiastically hear about her dates and humbly give counsel where needed.

Not only do we have to make lifestyle changes, but our *other children* have to also. This was difficult for us. We should have prayed and prepared more for this, recognizing that each sibling would process the new relationship differently. We should have talked with our children and explained our expectations for how the courting couple will be treated. If we had shown godly leadership here, it would have been better for everyone involved (this includes not only siblings but extended family as well). This is one of the areas where we had to apologize, and we share it here for others to learn from our mistake.

Speaking of extended family, there is also the issue of the young man's family. Respect is key. The young man's parents are also going through a time of transition. Chances are that their view on relationships and their expectations will be different than ours. We can look for strengths in his parents and learn from them. We can serve the young couple by intentionally trying to build a friendship with his parents—maybe avoiding a discussion of "the kids." We can look for things we have in common and just have fun.

Warning: Our daughter's courtship can bring up unresolved issues in our own marriage.

Mom: Chris hasn't come over much lately.

Dad: Yeah, he's probably busy.

Mom: Well, I think it's starting to affect Rasheda.
She seems a little downcast.

Dad: It's January. The playoffs.
He'll probably start coming over more after the Super Bowl.

(A loud silence fills the room until Dad finally looks
up from the computer and sees his wife's face.)

Dad: It's just another week....

Mom: Don't you think he's being inconsiderate to Rasheda?
Expecting her to be there whenever he feels like coming over, but
then expecting her to understand if he has better things to do?

Dad: Honey, it is Super Bowl season. It's only once a year.

Mom: You don't think this is a big deal, do you? You know why? Because you are the same way! You expect me to jump through hoops to make dinner for the kids and arrange babysitting at the drop of a hat just because you suddenly feel like going out to eat. I would like some consistency, like a weekly date night. And that's what Rasheda would like too!

Parents, can you feel the tension? We had many conversations like this while our daughter Brittany was courting Daniel. Not revolving around football specifically, but involving areas where Mary Lou felt Daniel was not responding well, and I thought it was no big deal.

For wives especially the way their husbands evaluate young men can reveal a lot about what their husbands think is important—and this may differ drastically from what the wives feel is important. A wife can battle fear as she identifies weaknesses in the young suitor that are similar to her husband's, knowing how painful those weaknesses can play out in a marriage. The bottom line is this: our wives don't want our daughters to get hurt.

Men, our wives need compassion during this emotional time, but they also need our leadership. As is our temptation since the days of Adam, we may tend to let our wives lead us and overreact to weaknesses in the young man. It is important to intentionally separate our marriage from the young couple and not let them suffer for our arguments. We must also listen to what our wives are saying. God may be using our daughter's courtship to reveal areas in our own marriages that are painful and need to be healed.

Dad: Honey, do you really want to have weekly date nights? I thought you were too busy at night.

Mom: I would love to have a night to look forward to each week.

Dad: Okay, I'll do what I can and rearrange my schedule. Let's start tomorrow. But you know what? I don't really think that Chris is

*being inconsiderate. Maybe he and Rasheda need to talk about their
expectations. Why don't you encourage Rasheda to tell Chris how she
feels and give him a chance to respond before we jump to conclusions?*

We had to repent to the Lord and to Brittany and Daniel for letting
our marital conflicts spill over into our relationship with them. Mary Lou
repented for letting fear rule her heart, and I repented for not leading
well. We are thankful for forgiveness, and we are delighted that we have
wonderful relationships with them now.

Strategies for Victory

How can you help your daughter have a God-honoring relationship
with a young man? Here is a re-cap of some of the areas we've discussed
and some additional strategies for victory:

- **Help your daughter feel loved and valued.** Give her the
  expectation of being treated well and the confidence to avoid
  young men that tear her down.

- **Help your daughter understand how much God loves her and
  pray that she will understand the magnitude of His love for
  her.**

- **Teach your daughter that every relationship matters to the
  Lord and that He gives commands for the way we treat others.**
  Embracing these standards in all relationships will help her walk
  in virtue with young men and stay far away from compromise.

- **Watch out for conflicts that arise in your own marriage.** See
  the areas of weakness in your marriage that are revealed and seek
  the Lord for healing. Don't let your marital conflicts hinder the
  young couple.

- **Explain that dating from one person to another is practicing
  for divorce.** In *The Family—God's Weapon for Victory*, the author

states, "An aspect of the dating syndrome of going steady and then breaking up, and going steady and breaking up ad infinitum, is that the ending of emotional attachments gets to be commonplace. What was difficult to do the first time gets to be, if not easier, at least more familiar, with each occurrence. We learn that emotional bonds are not permanent, because we've had a dozen of them! Marriage, on the other hand, demands perseverance in the face of tremendous adversity."[11]

- **Talk with your daughter about what she admires in men, help her understand what qualities are important to God, and help your daughter see where she needs to grow to better complement her future husband.**

Dannah Gresh, author of the book *And the Bride Wore White*, recommends writing down the qualities desired in a husband.[12] This can be a helpful tool when emotions run high and common sense runs low. For example, look at this warning from Ann Dunagan in *The Mission-Minded Family*: "One of the biggest hindrances to a young person fulfilling his or her calling to missions is marrying someone—even someone who is nice and loves the Lord—who is not also called to world missions."[13] A list that your daughter makes herself can help her evaluate the young men more sensibly and keep focused on the things she feels the Lord has placed on her heart.

- Psalm 37:4 says, "Delight yourself in the Lord and He will give you the desires of your heart." **As your daughter gets older, continue to help her delight in the Lord and respect the desires of her heart.** As you are aware of your daughter's heart and keep the lines of communication open, it will be easier to recognize when a potential husband enters the scene.

Your involvement as a father is priceless here. Let's be honest: men know men. We can smell a "player" from miles away. We remember what it's like to be young with raging hormones. We can be a helpful and protective force during this uncertain time.

A father can meet with the young man privately to get to know him better and ferret out issues that are best handled man to man. It's good to discuss his past, his present, and his future. This can serve everyone as we help the young man see if there are any harmful patterns that could be addressed now and help him to evaluate his life to see if he is indeed ready for marriage and specifically ready for marriage to our daughter.

A book that has been helpful to me is *What He Must Be…If He Wants To Marry My Daughter* by Voddie Baucham, Jr.[14] I (Rich) led a group of young men through this study and one ended up marrying my daughter and one ended up marrying a close friend's daughter. If we can help a young man evaluate himself biblically, we are serving him and his future family.

- **Meet with both young people and discuss guidelines.** Will there be limits on how often the young couple talk or see each other? Will they go places alone or bring along a sibling? What about limits on physical affection? Hand-holding, hugging, kissing, where will the line be drawn? A commitment from everyone is helpful as the relationship is dedicated to the Lord for His purposes with the desire to treat each other with honor.

- **We need to ask questions and help our daughter and her boyfriend evaluate issues according to Scripture.** A courtship is a delicate balance between *equipping* the young man and *evaluating* the young man. Our input can help him grow in the Lord as we bring up topics that may be new to him, but since he is not married to our daughter yet, it is the time to evaluate whether this relationship should lead to marriage. This is a wonderful time for lots of prayer as we seek God's best for our daughter.

Our friends are helping their young adult daughter walk in a relationship with a man she met through international missions work. He's a great guy, but the challenge is he lives in another country. The mom, Shawnie, says this: "We keep the lines of communication open and we Skype with him weekly. Our goal is not to protect them from conflicts, but to teach our daughter how to evaluate. We don't take sides; we are for both of them. We try to help our daughter decide if a difference is a deal breaker and we give him room to grow. Our daughter wants us involved in their lives and we would love to be some of the people they turn to for counsel if they get married."

A New Son

In many ways, we have spent a lifetime setting aside our own feelings to serve our daughter, and this season can be the hardest test of that love. We shouldn't be surprised, though. We knew this day was coming the first time we held her in our arms.

And if this is the time to release her into marriage, we see that our arms are not left empty. We look down and see quite the opposite. Our arms, and our hearts, are fuller. The Lord has added another...another to treasure...another to pray for...another to enjoy...another to laugh with...another to learn from...another to love. A son-in-law.

We now have a new son to love...forever! The young man that was once coming to visit is now here to stay. And though our lives will change, we will discover many new adventures awaiting our family as this new member brings his unique interests, passions, and talents. He will forever change the dynamic of our family, but we can face the future with joy and expectation as we commit to support our daughter and her husband and the new family they will build.

Prayer

Lord, I pray that you would give us a vision for preparing our daughter for marriage. May we work diligently to help her grow in the qualities that she will need as a wife. May our involvement in the process of her transitioning from singleness to marriage be a huge blessing to her and her future husband. And please shape and mature our daughter's future husband into a mighty man of God that will be able to effectively lead her and love her in a way that honors You.

---

[1] Joshua Harris, *I Kissed Dating Goodbye* (Colorado Springs: Multnomah Books, 2003).
[2] www.cslewis.org, accessed 1 May 2015.
[3] Stormie Omartian, *Lord, I Want To Be Whole* (Nashville: Thomas Nelson, Inc., 2001).
[4] Joshua Harris, *I Kissed Dating Goodbye* (Colorado Springs: Multnomah Books, 2003) 19.
[5] Colossians 3:8; Colossians 3:12; Ephesians 6:18; Hebrews 3:13; Romans 12:17; 1 Corinthians 13:4; Philippians 2:3-4; 1 John 1:7; Romans 13:14; 1 Corinthians 8:9.
[6] *Webster's Dictionary of the English Language*, s.v. "virtue."
[7] Dale Carnegie, *How to Win Friends and Influence People* (New York: Pocket Books, 1998).
[8] John Eldredge, *Wild at Heart* (Nashville: Thomas Nelson, Inc., 2011).
[9] Janet Benge and Geoff Benge, *Hudson Taylor: Deep in the Heart of China* (Seattle: YWAM, 1998).
[10] Anna Sofia Botkin and Elizabeth Botkin, *It's (Not That) Complicated* (Centerville, TN: The Western Conservatory of the Arts and Sciences, 2011) 69.
[11] Robert Andrews, *The Family: God's Weapon for Victory* (Rice, WA: Sentinel Press, 1995) 233.
[12] Dannah Gresh, *And the Bride Wore White* (Chicago: Moody Publishers, 2004).
[13] Ann Dunagan, *The Mission-Minded Family* (Colorado Springs: Authentic Publishing, 2007) 181.
[14] Voddie Baucham, Jr. *What He Must Be...If He Wants to Marry My Daughter* (Wheaton, IL: Crossway Books, 2009).

The Daughters Speak

Brittany Says...

When I first got this chapter to edit, I was very curious to read it because I am the only one of my sisters who has had a boyfriend and gotten married. And I wanted to know what my parents said! Reading this chapter actually brought up a whole lot of good memories.

Growing up in middle and high school, friends were always welcome at our place. I loved bringing people over and knew that my parents would always be hospitable and set an extra place (or seven!) for spontaneous friends my sisters and I brought home. I even remember coming home late at night and sneaking around because we had girls on the couch and in my bed as I tried to fumble for a light to see who they were!

Because of that I never felt like I needed to go out alone with friends all the time, guys or girls. We had much more fun at my house playing speed scrabble, acting games, and whatnot. Many times if I was invited out with friends my age I would grow bored because they always sat around and never knew what to do. Many times I would suggest they just all come back to my house because there was more than enough to do there!

All my guy and girl friends respected my parents and loved talking with them. Almost every guy that came over would end up staying late and talking with my dad. I always felt safe knowing that my dad knew who my guy friends were and communicated with most of them regularly.

Having guys at our house often helped me evaluate a guy a lot better than if I was alone with him or in a group of people our own age. I was able to see how he interacted with my siblings and whether or not he was kind to them. Having a large family was important to me, so guys who couldn't handle kids were crossed off the list!

I also was able to evaluate their communication skills as they talked with my parents or people of varying ages. As we all talked, it gave me better insight into their strengths and what their dreams and goals were. Because there were always other people around, there were never awkward pauses in conversations because there were usually several people ready to ask a question or interject if the other took a breath.

It wasn't only fun and games at our house though. We regularly went out evangelizing or had prayer meetings. These weekly times were a great glimpse into the guy's spiritual life. In the beginning a lot of them were not super comfortable with big prayer meetings or evangelizing with strangers, which was totally okay with me. What was amazing was to see how, as time progressed, they got so much better and grew in their boldness. That was always encouraging to me because I was never looking for someone perfect, but rather someone who was humble enough to recognize his need to grow and then embrace change.

My parents each had different roles during this season. My mom always had food and never turned friends away. She is a very good listener and my friends would pour their hearts out to her and receive advice. My dad was the conversationalist who would talk to everyone and ask questions. He would also keep the games or whatever we were doing moving along so everyone could participate and no one would be left out.

A memory from Father's Day stands out to me. Several of our friends dropped by the house and were still there when it came time for us to go around the room and honor my dad. One of the young men, recently married with a newly pregnant wife, asked if he could share. He talked about being in our home, seeing my dad in fun situations or stressful situations, and watching in amazement as my dad seemed to effortlessly love on his children and always make time for them. With tears in his eyes he said, "I know that you weren't a Christian growing up and did lots of wrong things. But to see you now as a dad and a husband gives me hope for my future. If God can do these things in you, He can do them in me."

I knew that my dad had influenced lots of young men over the years, but hearing it from someone else reiterated how important those times are. Just think about what a difference you as parents can make in the lives of your daughter's friends! A lot of them have grown up in dysfunctional families and you may be the spiritual mom and dad they need. And who knows, one of them may become your son-in-law!

8

There Goes My Girl

Preparing and Launching Your Arrow

What metaphor best describes your daughter?

Do you see her as a beautiful ring on your hand...that makes you look good?

Do you see her as a pebble in your shoe...tolerable but difficult to endure for long periods of time?

Do you see her as a flower in your garden...whose main purpose is to make you happy?

Do you see her as a thorn in your side...irritating and hindering your freedom?

Do you see her as a servant...created to work around the house so you can pursue your own hobbies?

Do you see her as a sports car...smart and fun to show off to your friends?

How we view our daughter affects everything we do. We've already established that she is a gift from God, but what type of gift? At a party, we may get lots of gifts, but each is a different item. What is a daughter? When you open her up, when you get to know her, what do you discover that she is? What does God, who gave you this gift, say that she is?

Behold, children are a gift of the Lord, the fruit of the womb is a reward.
Like arrows in the hand of a warrior, so are the children of one's youth.
Psalm 127:3-4

Like what?
Arrows.
Really? My daughter is an arrow?
Yes, she is.
But why do I need an arrow?
Because *you* are a warrior!
A warrior? No, I'm a banker. I'm a dentist. I'm a housewife. I'm a
computer programmer.
Arrows are given to warriors.
Well, if I'm a warrior, what war am I in?

Remember 1 Peter 5:8: our enemy is roaring like a lion looking to devour us. And what about Ephesians 6:12: "For our struggle is not against flesh and blood, but against the rulers, against the powers, against the world forces of this darkness, against the spiritual forces of wickedness in the heavenly places."

Oswald J. Smith said, "The Body of Christ is not a pleasure cruiser on its way to Heaven, but a battleship stationed at the very gates of Hell."[1]

Consider God's mysterious design. We become Christians, babes in the Lord. But where are we to grow up? Where are we to mature and be strengthened? Right smack in enemy territory!

Satan is described in 2 Corinthians 4:4 as the god of this world, yet we know from Psalm 24:1 that the earth is the Lord's and everything in it. Oh, it's a battlefield, my friend. Don't believe it yet? Just flip through a history book and see the stories of greed and torture play out over the annals of time as heroic men and women rose up to push back the advancement of evil. Or just open up today's newspaper. There the battle is played out in every town, every school, and every business.

We will one day be in a place with no suffering and no tears. A place where perfect love and joy abounds—but that's where we end up, not where we start. We start right here on earth, in the middle of a war.

And if there is a war going on, there are armies. Whose army are we in? We are in the Lord's army.

Okay, I see that we are in a war and that I'm in the Lord's army. But where is the battle? Where am I supposed to be fighting?

Here's the answer: what are your passions? You are fearfully and wonderfully made by the creator of the world. What unique passions has He placed in your heart?

Evangelism, abolishing abortion, ending the sex slave trade, caring for the elderly, feeding the poor, rescuing orphans, praying, showing Christ's love through hospitality...the options are endless. What about battling to protect our families, to preserve Scripture, to retain our freedom to assemble?

This ain't heaven—the battles are everywhere.

Picture this: We are warriors. The battles are raging all around us. There is smoke, confusion. We see casualties strewn throughout our land, and we cling to news of victories. We feel the heat, we see the enemy coming towards us.

And God reaches down and hands us an arrow.

How do we respond?

Ugh, what's this bulky thing?...I'll put it back here in my quiver... Ouch, what a pain, it pokes me while I run and it slows me down...What? God has given me another one, and another? Come on, they look impressive, but they're getting harder to carry. I could move much better without this weight on my back. I think God wants me to be free so I can really fight.

Though we may not use these words, is this how we are tempted to view our children?

It *is* difficult to be responsible for another person. Our children slow us down, and we have to say no to some opportunities. And it's true, our children do sometimes poke us and hurt us.

But the man or woman who sees the battle raging and knows he/she is a warrior has only one response when handed an arrow: *Thank you, God!*

Fill my quiver!

"Behold, children are a gift of the Lord, the fruit of the womb is a reward. Like arrows in the hand of a warrior, so are the children of one's youth. *How blessed is the man whose quiver is full of them; they will not be ashamed when they speak with their enemies in the gate*" (Ps. 127:3-5, emphasis added).

Do you see the confidence in this man? He is not ashamed when he speaks with his *enemies*. For he knows he has arrows from the Lord.

Take a moment. Have you forgotten that you have an arrow in your quiver? Are you walking hunched over by the burden of parenting instead of striding upright with the boldness of a warrior that is well equipped? Have you been complaining about the point that sometimes jabs you instead of rejoicing in your sharp weapon and strategizing how your arrow can do some damage to the enemy camp?

When you come home from work, you are not entering a building only meant to provide meals, lodging, and places to sit in front of a few TV's and computers. You are entering an armory. A strategic facility where rough arrows are sharpened and straightened for the battle. A place where sins and lies are whittled off, and truths and power are molded on the arrowhead.

When you wake up in the morning, you are not facing another day of the same ol' same ol'. You have a new day to fashion your arrow, to strengthen your arrow, to pray for your arrow. You have been given a weapon of warfare, and it is your job to prepare it for launch. Every decision we make about our home—what we allow in, who we allow in, how we spend our time, how we spend our money—all of these decisions should be made in light of this purpose.

Following Our Commander's Directions

We have been parenting for over two decades, and let us warn you: encouragement and equipping will not come from the world. Working in God's armory can be a lonely job.

Think about your past week. Who thanked you for buying food for your daughter? Who cheered you on when your daughter threw her tenth temper tantrum of the week and you still responded patiently? Who gave you a hug for even getting out of bed and facing a day that you knew would be brutal? Who patted you on the back when you stood your ground while your thirteen-year-old pouted and reminded you that you are the strictest parent in the *whole* world?

For many of us, encouragement is rare. Societal forces diminish the importance of parents, relegating us to out-of-touch old folks that don't understand today's youth and whose primary function is to provide for the material needs of our daughters.

Is that really all we are? A source of provision while our daughters grow up being molded by the leaders and institutions of society? No, we have been given God's girl to raise in His way, with His power, for His purposes. *To raise our children for the glory of God, we must first understand and embrace our calling as parents.* We must see that these beautiful gifts from God are arrows, and that we need to raise them as such.

When we start a new job, we don't stroll into the office, plop down at the computer, and start typing and creating whatever documents we want. We first must look at the job description, understand what is expected of us, and then learn from our supervisor and co-workers. We must know the mission of the company and our role in that mission. When we understand our purpose and our contribution, then we are better equipped to fulfill our position and excel in our job.

The same is true with the job of parenting, the job of sharpening our arrows. We cannot take our little girl and decide how we want to raise her. We must follow the manual provided by the owner and creator of the universe—the owner and creator of our daughter.

Scripture = Truth

Second Timothy 3:16-17 says, "All Scripture is inspired by God and profitable for teaching, for reproof, for correction, for training in righteousness; that the man of God may be adequate, equipped for every good work." Is raising our daughter for the Lord a good work? Yes. How do we get equipped? By following the Scriptures.

To follow Scripture, we must know Scripture. And parenting is much easier when our children are learning the Scriptures with us. An excellent resource for this is the *Sword Study Series*.[2] These books are written especially for families to study a particular book of the Bible together, pray through the truths learned, memorize Scriptures, and have fun in the process. For each book of the Bible studied, there are five different academic levels to choose from that perfectly parallel each other in scope but differ in depth, so that everyone is studying the same thing at the same time, just at different intensities. We've set apart time in the summer for many years to do the *Sword Study Series,* and our lives, and family unity, have been greatly enriched.

As we study, we will discover there are times when our opinions are different than Scripture; when we don't agree with something in the Bible or we just don't feel like obeying. What do we do then? Well, if we call ourselves Christians, that means we are followers of Christ. And how did Christ live? In John 14:31a, Jesus says, "But so that the world may know that I love the Father, I do exactly as the Father commanded Me."

So, as Christians, we must obey God. When our opinion differs from Scripture, we must bow down and be changed by the timeless truths of God's Word. We must check all parenting advice against the Word of God. *We can't expect God to bless our efforts if we're not following His directions.* If Jesus is Lord of our lives, He is Lord of our parenting.

What *is* important to God? What should we focus on as we sharpen our arrows? Does He say that our daughter's education is primary and that we should invest our best time and energy in helping her succeed academically? Does God say that a clean room is next to godliness? What about sports? Should our daughter's performance on the soccer field be our focus as we spend our time together practicing and preparing for games? Nothing is wrong with any of these, but are they *most* important?

Before we even answer this, let's ask another question: what would our daughter say is most important to us? She will come to her conclusion from our words, our reactions, and our investments. What would she say is most important to us? Now might be a good time to ask her. Do the priorities that we project upon our daughter align with the Word of God?

God doesn't focus on the grades, chores, or field performance; He looks at the heart. First Samuel 16:7 says, "But the Lord said to Samuel, 'Do not look at his appearance or at the height of his stature, because I have rejected him; for God sees not as man sees, for man looks at the outward appearance, but the Lord looks at the heart.'"

If the heart is most important to God, then it needs to be most important to us as we sharpen our arrows.

Sharpening Our Arrows

While we are clearly called to enjoy and treasure our sweet daughters, we must keep in mind that they are arrows from the Lord. Part of our responsibility as parents is to prepare these weapons for battle. Here are some directives from our Commander-in-Chief and how we can apply them to parenting:

Discipline our daughters diligently

Proverbs 13:24 — "He who withholds his rod hates his son, but he who loves him disciplines him diligently."

Train our daughters to guard their hearts and minds

Psalm 101:2-3a — "I will be careful to lead a blameless life—when will you come to me? I will walk in my house with blameless heart. I will set before my eyes no vile thing" (NIV).

Proverbs 4:23 — "Watch over your heart with all diligence, for from it flow the springs of life."

Spend lots of time with our daughters, teaching them about God

Deuteronomy 6:6-8 — "These words, which I am commanding you today, shall be on your heart. You shall teach them diligently to your sons and shall talk of them when you sit in your house and when you walk by the way and when you lie down and when you rise up. You shall bind them as a sign on your hand and they shall be as frontals on your forehead."

Know our giftings and our passions and include our daughters in our ministries

1 Peter 4:10 — "As each one has received a special gift, employ it in serving one another as good stewards of the manifold grace of God."

Seize opportunities

Ephesians 5:15-16 — "Therefore be careful how you walk, not as unwise men but as wise, making the most of your time, because the days are evil."

Give them opportunities to rise up

1 Corinthians 16:13-14 — "Be on the alert, stand firm in the faith, act like men, be strong. Let all that you do be done in love."

Pray for our daughters like Epaphras

Colossians 4:12 — "Epaphras, who is one of you and a servant of Christ Jesus, sends greetings. He is always wrestling in prayer for you, that you may stand firm in all the will of God, mature and fully assured" (NIV).

Seek counsel in our parenting

Proverbs 10:17 — "He who heeds discipline shows the way to life, but whoever ignores correction leads others astray" (NIV).

Proverbs 12:1 — "Whoever loves discipline loves knowledge, but he who hates correction is stupid" (NIV).

Maintain intimacy with the Lord so that we will bear good fruit

John 15:5-8 — "I am the vine, you are the branches; he who abides in Me and I in him, he bears much fruit, for apart from Me you can do nothing. If anyone does not abide in Me, he is thrown away as a branch and dries up; and they gather them, and cast them into the fire and they are burned. If you abide in Me, and My words abide in you, ask whatever you wish, and it will be done for you. My Father is glorified by this, that you bear much fruit, and so prove to be My disciples."

Aiming Our Arrows

Each daughter, each arrow, has different giftings and strengths. One of our roles as parents is to help identify these abilities and enhance them. Here are some tools to help identify and develop our daughters' strengths:

Surround Them with Powerful Role Models

- Invite missionaries, government leaders, successful entrepreneurs, abolitionists, and pastors over for dinner. Look for whom God brings into our lives and learn from them. We can keep the conversation appropriate for our daughters' ages and encourage them to ask questions.

- Keep our bookshelves stocked with biographies of inventors, pioneers, restaurant founders, scientists, missionaries, and doctors. A family read-a-loud can open up excellent dialogue.

- Observe our daughters. What careers and what stories excite them? Who do they bring up in conversation or whom do they respect?

In our drawer we have a wrinkled notebook paper that is older than a decade. A handwritten list of twenty-five people. Names that Brittany had written down after talking to her sisters. The title of the paper, written in her twelve-year-old print, is "People We Want to Have Over."

We had been taught that practicing hospitality was vital to the health of our family and church body. Our girls grew up with a weekly Bible study meeting in our home, family friends visiting a couple times a week, and one new family or single person being invited over every week.

Then Rich and I hit a difficult season in our lives. We suddenly faced many logistical and relational struggles. Rich felt unprepared and fearful of his increased responsibilities. I felt overwhelmed and under-loved. And we stopped inviting people over. We were consumed by our own problems.

But we had taught our daughters that practicing hospitality was a command from the Lord. Our older girls could read Scripture. They knew what God required of us. And so they asked, gently, every once in a while, if we could invite someone over for dinner or dessert or anything.

"No," Rich and I would respond, with glazed eyes and weary bodies. "Now is not a good time."

Then one day, they handed us the list—twenty-five people our daughters wanted to invite to our home. There it was in writing. Our daughters' appeal, simple, yet so convicting. To us, this one piece of paper was a cry out from our daughters: "We want to obey Scripture. Please help us."

We were humbled. And here is yet another way that our daughters are a gift from God. As we teach them God's ways, they can then rise up and challenge us to obey when we are struggling. A family of God—helping and encouraging each other, regardless of age.

Pursue Serving Opportunities

- Where does our church need help? Children's ministry, administration, lawn care, painting, greeting, or food pantry? We can jump in and bring our daughters alongside us when they are young and then encourage them to serve independently as they mature.

- Ask a trusted friend to include our daughters in their ministries. Do we have a friend that delivers meals to the elderly, hands out water bottles to the homeless, knits hats for premature babies, or cleans homes for new mothers? Look for ways that our friends can increase our daughters' experiences and draw from their expertise.

- We can watch and ask questions to discover what our daughters enjoy and how they are gifted.

And then, we need to let them walk in that gifting. Oh, that can be the hardest.

Becky shares at the end of this chapter her perspective on wanting to go to the mission field, and me (Mary Lou) not being enthusiastic. She brought me correction, and it was exactly what I needed.

There is no doubt in my mind that Becky is called by God to spread the gospel. She has faithfully made her hometown her mission field. Actually, everywhere she goes, physically or through cyberspace, becomes an opportunity to share God's love. She stops and prays for people in the spaghetti aisle, listens to the needs of restaurant hostesses, scrolls Facebook to see who God wants her to send an encouraging word to, and buys Bibles for those she meets who have none.

Many people have confirmed that Becky is called to a life of missions in foreign lands. *But for her to go, I must release.* All our teaching about obeying and trusting God can come to a head when we are challenged to let our daughters go and obey God.

It's not just sending them out to a foreign country that's scary. It's scary to let your daughter go to a gymnastics competition. It's scary when your daughter wants to try out for a musical—and she might not be chosen. It's scary to have a daughter marry a man who plans to live on the other side of the country. It's scary to let your daughter go to college and be exposed to the many traps of the enemy. It's scary when your daughter wants to share the gospel with the girls in her fourth grade class.

We have encouraged our daughters to grow in faith throughout their lives. The irony is that they often become the catalyst that helps our own faith grow as we see God's hand in their lives and cry out for the courage to let our precious girls walk in their giftings. We pour into them, and then as they mature, they often pull us along.

Give Our Daughters Responsibilities and Expect Them to Rise Up

- Let our daughters plan the meals, design a room, write the annual Christmas letter, host a fund-raiser, plant a garden, or start a Bible study.

- We can give gentle support, but let's avoid smothering them with our ideas and preferences. It's all right if they do things differently than we do.

- What does our daughter excel at? Keep giving her opportunities to develop her skills and gain confidence. Her gifting will soon become clear.

"Mom, would it help if I took over planning and cooking the meals while you are writing the book?" Beautiful words from our youngest daughter. My answer was clear and precise: "Oh, yes! Thank you so much!"

Has Stephanie served perfectly balanced meals every day and followed my recipes? Certainly not. When I said yes, it was with a thankful heart, but I also knew it needed to be with a supportive heart. I gave her freedom to cook whatever she wanted. Stephanie's desire is to serve, and that is pleasing to the Lord. It's a great opportunity for her to find joy in serving her family, trying new recipes, and preparing to one day run her own home. The family has loved her new cooking ideas, and I have been blessed by the temporary reprieve in my schedule.

Our sweet Stephanie often gets asked the question, "What do you want to do when you graduate?" She earned a college scholarship at the age of fifteen. She faithfully babysits for us and other families, works as a marketing assistant, teaches children on Sunday morning, runs her own online business, and has written an e-book. All this while being eager to jump in with whatever her sisters or brothers are doing, anything from going blueberry picking, to playing football, to helping color her sister's hair. Her talents are wide and her enthusiasm strong.

But we've learned to not ask the question, "What do you want to do when you graduate?" We've learned to ask instead, "What do you believe God wants you to do?" That can be completely different.

As we write this, our home is a bustle of activity. Stephanie, and our whole family, has been seeking the Lord about what He would like her to do next. Suddenly, a door flew open for her. She was accepted as a summer intern at an international Christian ministry. Stephanie is delighted, and we are very encouraged as we watched her lay down her own will through prayer and lift up a cry to God: "Lord, I want to be where you want me to be."

Yes, when we delight ourselves in the Lord, He gives us the desires of our hearts. As we love God, our desires are shaped by Him. But, let's be honest. If someone asked me (Mary Lou) what I would like to be doing today, I'd reply: "I'd like to be sitting by the pool with a stack of great books and a pitcher of cold iced tea." That's what I'd like, but that's not what God has called me to.

When I embrace what God has called me to, I discover great joy in obeying Him. And that's what we want our daughters to know too.

Launching Our Arrows

We have sharp arrows that are well aimed. It is now time to launch. Thankfully, God has us launch our arrows a little at a time: go on a short-term mission trip, stay with a busy young mom while her husband is out of town, work for a local business, or travel with a summer choir group. All of these are preparing our daughters, *and us,* for what the future will hold as they become young adults and we launch our arrows for the final time.

A funny thing happens while we are preparing and launching our arrows; God is often preparing and launching us.

Our friends, Joe and Shawnie, have led missionary teams to Honduras for many years. They are on the board of directors of a Honduras ministry. How did they become so devoted to this country and its people?

It began when their ten-year-old daughter came home from school talking about a boy who had shared in class about his recent missionary trip. After excitedly telling Joe and Shawnie all the details, their daughter simply said, "I'm supposed to be a missionary."

Her father responded to this request and soon took her on a missionary trip to Honduras. She loved it and loved the people they served. They began going regularly. Eventually, Shawnie started joining them on the trips. "I wanted to experience what my daughter loved," she says.

Their daughter traveled the world sharing the gospel through YWAM, a large Christian outreach organization, and was even on staff by the age of twenty-one. When people hear about her and ask her mom how she instilled in her daughter a love for missions, Shawnie's answer is simple: "We didn't give her a love for missions and outreach; she gave it to us."

The Final Launch

And then, that day will come. The day when you take this daughter you love so dearly, this daughter you have sacrificed for, this daughter that you treasure, and you set her in your bow and launch her out one last time. That day will come dear parents, quicker than you think. You may be sending her off in marriage or sending her off to begin a new assignment from God.

When that day comes, her life will dramatically change, but so will ours. It's a turning of the page.

We stand there, watching her go, memories flooding our minds and tears rolling down our faces. The day we first laid eyes on that girl, a part of our heart was ripped out and placed in her. And now she is walking away, with that piece of our heart. What does her future hold? Life can be hard and people can be mean. Will our little girl be okay?

In this moment, the Lord puts His arm around us in a comforting embrace—an embrace that can only come from a Father who knows what it's like to send off a beloved child into a harsh world.

We remember the laughter and the pain. The mistakes and the victories. The battles and the repenting. The prayers and the pleadings. The hugs, the smiles, the dolls, the dancing, the late night talks, the times at the parks. The years come tumbling through our mind, and then...they end.

We have raised our daughter. And although we will always love her and be a part of her life, our responsibility to train her up in the Lord has ended. Our assignment is complete.

We stand with the One who gave us this precious girl, and we launch her out in His name. As we lean into our Lord's strong arms and watch our daughter slowly fade from sight, may we hear these precious words whispered in our ears: "*Well done, good and faithful servant. Well done.*"

Prayer

Lord, thank You for the time that You have given us with our daughter. Help us to be faithful in preparing her to be launched, and help us to be teachable as You use her gifts and strengths to challenge us to grow. As we release her to the work that You have called her to do, may she go forth in great faith and confidence in Your amazing love and awesome power.

---

[1] Ray Comfort, "Militant Evangelism," *Way of the Master* video series, May 5, 2015.
[2] Tammy McMahan, *Sword Study Series,* (Clarksville: Word in the Family Ministries, 2015).

The Daughters Speak

Becky Says...

So I may not be the typical American girl. At age three I had given my life to Jesus, by age six I was determined God had called me to be a missionary to China, and at age nine I decided I would go to unreached people groups and share Jesus no matter the cost.

When most children would be playing cops and robbers, I would gather my sisters and friends to play cops and missionaries. I assigned a few kids the role of the "bad guys" or "cops," and then the rest of the children and myself would be the missionaries running away from the cops and trying to keep our Bibles hidden.

My heroes weren't Super Girl or Batman, but Gladys Aylward and Hudson Taylor. I would dream of the day I would go to China and rescue hundreds of little children or bring the gospel into prisons and be martyred for my faith. Dying in bed as an old lady in a nursing home sounded so miserably unadventurous, but being martyred for my faith in front of thousands of people in an overseas country—now that was the way to go!

Not one of my sisters or friends shared my dream at the time, but my parents always encouraged me to follow the path God had called me to. Even though I may have only been six-years-old, my parents were preparing to launch me. They never discouraged me from becoming a missionary, but encouraged me to learn Mandarin and study China. They also told me to make the city where we lived a mission field. They were sharpening their arrow (me)—getting me ready to be launched.

Then suddenly it was time to be launched. I had been to a few places since graduating high school but was never gone longer than a month. But it was time. Time to go. My top choice was China, of course, but I was really open to anywhere the Lord called me to. I was ready. Ready to go. Ready to be launched.

But I felt resistance. Something holding me back. It wasn't God, and I didn't believe it was my dad. No, it was my mom. When I was a child, Mom had always been encouraging me to prepare to be a missionary, but when I became an adult, I felt resistance.

I felt as if I was a wild mustang trapped in a little barn stall, and just as the door was ready to break open, a tight rope was thrown around my neck making it difficult to run free.

Every time I mentioned going to China or any other place, my mom would say how she didn't want me to leave, or how much she would miss me. I couldn't talk to her about what I believed the Lord was calling me to, tell her my dreams and visions, or even ask her for help on practical things I had to get done before I left. I felt very alone. My dad was supportive, but there is something I think in every girl that wants her mom to be there too. I wanted her to be excited for me!

I was trapped. I had to go. I knew that was my calling, but I didn't want to go against my mom's wishes and hurt her. I know Jesus said no one is worthy of Him if he loves his father and mother more than Him (Matt. 10:37-38), but I knew my mom would hear from God and that she loved Him. It would have been different if she wasn't a Christian, but she was, and not only that, I respected her opinion and craved her approval. Now I would serve the Lord either way, if I had her approval or not, but I was hesitant because she does hear from the Lord, and I want to honor her.

I met with a pastor's wife at our church, and she encouraged me to talk to Mom about how I felt. I was very tentative at first but ended up bringing it to her attention a few weeks later. Mom explained she totally wanted me to go and do what God had called me to, but because of past experiences from her own life, she didn't want me to feel like she was kicking me out or was glad to get rid of me. She just wanted me to feel loved and know I will be *very* missed.

I was shocked! I couldn't have been more wrong about the judgments I made against her. I told her I totally felt loved by her and knew she would miss me. But I also explained that I want to feel her support too. She said she hadn't known I felt this way and that she would stop telling me she doesn't want me to go. That night she helped me get everything ready for a new passport, and I thanked her for the help and for how much she loves me.

Since that day she has changed the way she talks about my mission trips. She is my number one cheerleader and supporter! As one of my best friends, she is usually the first one I tell when I think God might be calling me somewhere new. I would not have been able to go to the places I have been without her! If it was Alaska, Middle East, or Southeast Asia she was right there for me.

I think many times parents fall to one side or the other. They either hold on to their children so tightly their children do not feel like they are able to walk down the path they are called, or the parents push them out so fast their kids feel all alone and abandoned.

I believe part of launching your children is being there by their side to encourage them along the way. I appreciate how my parents do not try to control my life but are there right by my side encouraging and challenging me to run the path God has called me to.

I think the number one thing young adults crave from their parents is encouragement. Encouragement about missions, school, work, relationships, marriage, etc. They want someone who will listen to them talk about their dreams and visions and, at times, their disappointments and pain. I know for me having my parents to encourage me along the way is one of the greatest blessings!

CLOSING TIME

"*Excuse me,*" *says the waitress as she deftly sweeps around our feet.*

We all look up, a little startled. A quick glance around the cafe' reveals staff members closing the blinds and wiping down the tables. Our watches confirm that our conversation about raising our daughters left us oblivious to the time.

"I guess we need to leave now."

We lay down a tip and start gathering our belongings.

"I wish we could meet like this every week."

"Yeah, I need the encouragement—and the challenge."

"I feel convicted where I have failed my daughter, but I also feel re-envisioned and empowered to raise her for the glory of God."

"It's so much easier to discuss parenting in a quiet café with fellow Christians committed to the Word of God. Real parenting is not like that. We are in the trenches every day with no one cheering us on from the sidelines. I need almost daily reminders of the importance of parenting."

"Yes, I want to remember that my daughter is a wonderful gift from God, and I want to raise her every day in His way, with His power, for His purposes."

"That's one of the challenges of biblical parenting. It's one of the most important jobs in the world, yet there are few sources of encouragement.

Meeting together tonight has been great, but we can't fit that into our schedule on an ongoing basis. How can we bring parenting encouragement into our home at our convenience?"

Fellow parents, this is how we often feel after we talk to other Christian parents or attend a parenting seminar. Envisioned and yearning to carry the enthusiasm into our ordinary lives.

One of the practices that has helped us so much is that we regularly read and discuss parenting books. It has been our experience that we can easily get distracted and overwhelmed by the daily responsibilities of raising our children and building a home, and yet quickly forget why we are doing what we're doing. Reading theologically strong books keeps the vision before us and provides an open platform for the Spirit of God to speak to us.

Discussing books as a couple has served us immensely. We each bring different strengths to our parenting, and discussing our viewpoints on issues and comparing our opinions to Scripture has strengthened our unity as parents and often revealed areas in our own minds that needed to be renewed with God's Word. Working to stand on the same parenting paradigm has been such a fruitful exercise over the years and has served our children well as they know that we are generally working as a team. God's design is that children should benefit from the assets of both a mother and a father, and by working things through together, we position ourselves to serve our daughters better.

There are many books we have read over and over. And each time, God highlights something new. Every year is a new season of parenting, and what we may not have been struggling with last year may suddenly crop up in surprising ways. Or we may be encouraged by the growth we've seen in ourselves, and in our daughters, by being reminded of former struggles that are now victories.

We find reading, or listening to, God-honoring books on Christian living to be like a refreshing waterfall as we fight our own tendencies towards laziness and selfishness. We only have a short time with our daughters and we want to lead them well with conviction, confidence, and courage. We are glad to have fellow Christians "sitting" on our bookshelves, waiting to encourage us.

We hope that this book has inspired and equipped you. We would love to meet you weekly at the café to cry together, learn from each other, and spur one another on to good works. While that is not possible, we pray that God has spoken to your heart as you've read this book. We would be delighted if you said this to a friend: "I just read a great book called *Raising God's Girl*. I can't remember who wrote it, but God spoke to me in so many specific ways as I was reading it. I wrote all over the margins as I tried to record the insights God gave me about my daughter, my parenting choices, and even my own heart. My daughter *is* a gift to me from God, and I am recommitted to doing *all* I can to raise her to be a strong young woman for Him."

If you are a dad reading this, we applaud you. Too often it is the women who read parenting books, and then they are left to try and apply what they've learned without their husbands' leadership and insights. If this book has been helpful to you, please recommend it to other dads.

No book replaces *The Bible*. It is the inspired, inerrant Word of God. It restores our souls and gives light to our paths (Ps. 19:7, 119:105). It is *the* official parenting book and all others should be evaluated by it. There is no other perfect book, including the one you're reading right now.

Throughout *Raising God's Girl* we have highlighted many books on Christian living that have equipped us over the years. We hope you will find them beneficial.

We are also including here a list of books that have encouraged and convicted us on our parenting journey. Not one of them is flawless, but each of them has highlighted a specific biblical truth. God has used these books to help us evaluate our parenting and build our convictions in such a way that we felt inspired to creatively and uniquely apply biblical truths in our family.

We are indebted to these authors for the investment they have made in our family. In most cases, we do not personally know the authors, so we can't vouch for their personal lives. But we can say God has used these books to convict us, envision us, and help us to be unified in our parenting. May they be a blessing to you too.

May the Lord bless you as you devote yourself to Raising God's Girl,
Rich and Mary Lou Graham

Recommended Resources

A Young Woman After God's Own Heart by Elizabeth George

Above Rubies Magazine by Nancy Campbell

Age of Opportunity: A Biblical Guide to Parenting by Paul David Tripp

And the Bride Wore White: Seven Secrets to Sexual Purity by Dannah Gresh

Before You Meet Prince Charming: A Guide to Radiant Purity by Sarah, Stephen, and Grace Mally

Character Matters!: Raising Kids with Values That Last by John and Susan Alexander Yates

Christian Heroes: Then & Now by Janet and Geoff Benge

Grooming the Next Generation for Success by Dani Johnson

Expecting Joy by Mary Lou Graham and Marianne Kelso

I Kissed Dating Goodbye by Joshua Harris

It's (Not That) Complicated: How to Relate to Guys in a Healthy, Sane, and Biblical Way by Anna Sofia Botkin and Elizabeth Botkin

Keeping Our Children's Hearts: Our Vital Priority by Steven and Teri Maxwell

Making Brothers and Sisters Best Friends by Sarah, Stephen, and Grace Mally

Raising Kids Who Hunger for God by Benny and Sheree Phillips

Shepherding a Child's Heart by Tedd Tripp

Sword Study Series by Tammy McMahan

The 5 Love Languages Series by Gary Chapman

The Duties of Parents by J.C. Ryle

The Family: God's Weapon for Victory by Robert Andrews

The Mission-Minded Family: Releasing Your Family to God's Destiny by Ann Dunagan

The Secret Keeper by Dannah Gresh

What He Must Be... If He Wants to Marry My Daughter by Voddie Baucham, Jr.

What the Bible Says About Child Training by Richard Fugate

Will Our Generation Speak? by Grace Mally

Need additional copies?

To order more copies of

RAISING *God's Girl*

contact Certa Publishing

☐ Order online at:
CertaBooks.com/RaisingGodsGirl

☐ Call 877-77-CERTA or

☐ Email Info@CertaPublishing.com